THE GREAT PORT ∂ BALTIMORE

Its First 300 Years

{ 1706–2006 }

By Helen Delich Bentley & F. Key Kidder

Special Thanks

or the last 60 years I have lived, breathed and battled for the Port of Baltimore. Credit my mother — my best friend, and the one who gave me the gift of her determination — for first stirring my interest in the Port through which she immigrated.

My mother, Mary Kovich Bjelich, and my father, Mane Ivanesevic, were immigrants; I well remember her stories of the trans-Atlantic voyage, being tossed about for 30 days in the bowels of a North German Lloyd steamship before finally setting foot in Baltimore. My mother's first husband, Sam Bjelich, was killed in a coal mining accident near Harrisburg, Pa.

After graduating from the University of Missouri on the very same day my mother became an American citizen, I started looking for a reporter's job anywhere — except the society page — in any city room on any eastern newspaper. I picked Baltimore only because the *Sunpapers'* Maclean Patterson offered me a paid one-way train ticket and $5 more pay a week. My editors were great: Ed Young and Bill Wells, who ran the City Desk, first suggested I go cover the Port "because we haven't had anyone there since before the war." Then, Charles H. "Buck" Dorsey, my Managing Editor, and Paul Banker, my City Editor who later succeeded Dorsey, enabled me to develop our maritime coverage into the nation's best.

At the same time I was at *The Sun*, Robert B. Cochrane, the No. 2 man at WMAR-TV, was instrumental in my documentary series, *"The Port That Built a City and State,"* which ran for 15 years and allowed me to really learn about the Port's prime role driving Maryland's industrial development. My TV team was the best — photographers Charles Purcell and Ed Eisenmeier, director Ray Ratajczak, film editor Irv Kemp and co-hosts Ad Weinert, George Rogers and Jack Dawson.

I parlayed my Baltimore media work — print and TV — into a syndicated column appearing in most of America's port city newspapers, which attracted the attention of Richard Nixon, who later appointed me Chairman of the Federal Maritime Commission.

In 1959, I married my wonderful Bill Bentley, so patient and ever willing to step back when the Port beckoned.

After voters of Maryland's Second Congressional District saw fit to elect me in 1985, I was able to spend a decade thumping for the Port and America's industrial base in Washington, D.C. And when I lost an election, Gov. William Donald Schaefer urged the Maryland Port Administration to take me on as a consultant. Today, the Port's staff is my family.

There are so many others: Jack Willis of Bethlehem; sponsors of my TV show including Frances and Willie Haussner, Capt. W. G. N. Rukert, Samuel Shapiro, Capt. Horace Jefferson and Bernie Rafferty; C.R. "Chick" Zarfoss of Western Maryland Railroad and Jervis Langdon of the B&O; ILA members and leaders Teddy Gleason, John Bowers, August Idzik, Jefferson Davis, John Kopp, William Haile, Ritchie Hughes and Horace Alston; customs inspectors like Jerry Dyer; immigration inspectors like Earl Steinberg; Coast Guard Capt. George McCabe; Capt. Prestley Carter of the Bay Pilots; Curtis Bay and Baker-Whitely tugboat captains. And to those I forgot and who now have a grudge, you know where to find me: at the Port.

Last but certainly not least, my thanks and credit go to those who helped provide art and photographs for the book: Jennifer Bodine, daughter of the late Aubrey Bodine; Annapolis-based maritime photographer Kathy Bergren Smith; the Baltimore Museum of Industry; the Maryland Historical Society; Vane Brothers, who lent their helicopter for aerial shots; and Patrick O'Brien, whose painting graces the cover.

Helen Delich Bentley

The world of maritime

has given me a great ride. To a little girl growing up in a small Nevada mining town, the oceans seemed as remote as the moon. Actually, the moon seemed closer; at least I could see it.

Although maritime commerce is the glue that binds today's global economy, I'll hazard the guess that Maryland's great Port of Baltimore — despite the fact that its vast operations sprawl over 40 miles of prime waterfront property — remains a remote and undervalued asset to most people in the state.

Why?

Because most of the Port's business is unseen; the only ones afforded a good glimpse are boaters on the Patapsco River or Chesapeake Bay.

It slips right past — like ships in the night, as they say.

So an increased general awareness of the Port's role is one of this book's primary objectives. The public has a need to know that the Port deposits money into the paychecks of 112,000 Maryland workers, satisfies the wants and needs of Maryland consumers, supplies statewide industry with raw materials and ready access to world markets, and richly rewards Maryland's tax base.

And the Port has a right for Maryland's citizens to know the difference it makes in their daily lives — 24/7/365.

A second objective of this book is educating Marylanders about the Port's incalculable economic value — past, present and future. As the Port's unofficial godmother, I hope you'll allow me to trot out my old television series, "The Port That Built a City and State," and amend it. Make that built, builds and will continue to build.

Visitors to the Inner Harbor in 1965, the year my series ended, didn't see shimmering Harborplace promenades along Pratt and Light streets. They saw docks, the working waterfront where it literally all began when Baltimore Town was founded in 1729.

Back then, the Port was pretty much all Baltimore had going for it. The story of Baltimore's emergence as a world-class city never would have been written without its world-class Port marching right in step alongside.

And when they write Maryland's history in another hundred years, it'll be more of the same, plus some.

Just thinking about the Port's future prospects makes this godmother think she better stick around to make sure they get it right.

Helen Delich Bentley

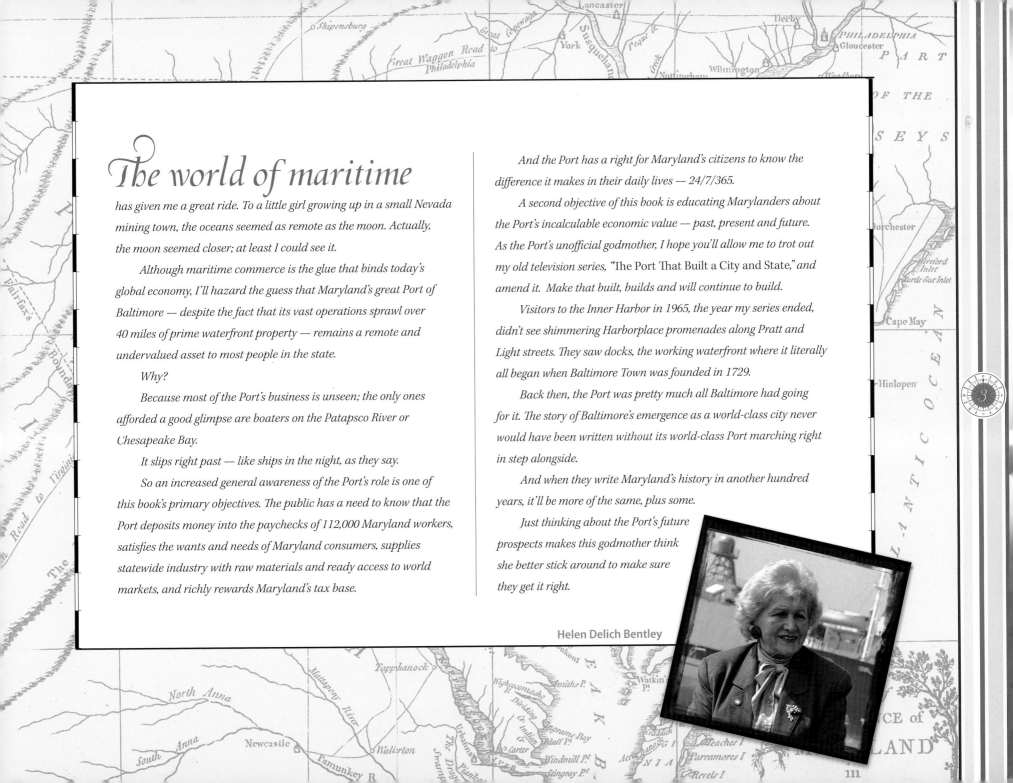

111

CONTENTS

History of the Port

Three-hundred years on the job without one hour off — that's 24/7/365 x 300 — is an enviable work history. And neither history nor work is in short supply on Baltimore's muscular waterfront, where ships and cargoes just keep getting bigger.

But the history of the Port of Baltimore does not stop at the water's edge. Then, as now, the Port's undercurrent surges beyond the docks, sweeps through downtown, and widens as it moves out across the state, bathing business and industry, washing over Maryland culture, engaging all through dozens of points of contact each and every day — even as most people outside the maritime community are clueless about an industry which is largely out of sight, and out of mind.

So the Port's history cannot be confined to waterfront fixtures which made it work so well for 300 years. Maritime's influence on the state and region is simply too vast, the impact of waterborne dollars too profound.

Old salts and storied ships have their place. But the truer telling of the Port's history embraces the concurrent development of metropolitan Baltimore and Maryland's counties — the beneficiaries of the Port's mission of economic development — and incorporates the Port's social and cultural legacy.

Without the Port, Baltimore as we know it would not exist. It would be something lesser and smaller. More likely, Baltimore would have died a quick death.

Colonial Maryland was no garden of leisure. It was a hard knock life, often short and brutal. Early attempts by Maryland settlers to establish towns honoring British founder Lord Baltimore (a.k.a. Cecil Calvert) on the Bush River in Harford County and the Eastern Shore quickly failed. Even after the third attempt finally took hold in 1724, on the marshlands where the Jones Falls empties into the Patapsco River, Baltimore was a garden-variety mud puddle in the wilderness.

Three decades later, Baltimore Town was hanging tough, but still hanging: in 1754, its inventory included a few hundred people, 24 houses, two taverns, one church — with a single finger pier stuck into the shallows.

Humble as it was, the finger pier was a difference-maker for Baltimore — that and its fortuitous proximity to the Patapsco River Valley, the cradle of Maryland's industrial revolution. The mutually beneficial relationship between the Port and industry was Baltimore's breath of life. Without their collaborative heft, Baltimore would have never approached its world-class status.

Baltimore Town wasn't Maryland's first official port; that honor belonged to Humphrey's Creek near Sparrows Point, which Colonial legislators designated a Port of Entry in 1687. Whetstone Point, near Fort McHenry, became Maryland's second Port of Entry 300 years ago in 1706 — the basis of the Port's 2006 Tricentennial celebration. Both ports trafficked in tobacco, Maryland's first cash crop.

Facing page: Containers await transport at Seagirt Marine Terminal, one of 35 public and private terminals serving the Port of Baltimore. The mass of the Port's sprawling facilities makes the better-known Inner Harbor seem downright diminutive.

Above: John Moale's 1752 depiction of the Port, looking north from Federal Hill.

Sotte Weed

The small island of Britain had, at the time, emerged as the world's greatest nation using an empire-building strategy dependent on getting what it wanted from nations it colonized, and what it wanted from Maryland was "sotte weed," as colonists called the leafy tobacco plant. The British developed a taste for tobacco from earlier explorations to the Caribbean. But America was closer, and the wealthy British investors who bankrolled the trans-Atlantic voyage of America's settlers did so convinced they would profit from the sale of Colonial tobacco to consumers in Europe, where the weed was worth its weight in silver — so precious it was smoked in narrow-stemmed pipes restricting its intake, and kept in blue Delft jars depicting Europeans' vision of "that innocente land" called America.

Britain ruled the world through sea power: While its navy played enforcer, the British merchant fleet freely hollowed out ripe stockpiles from far-flung ports — a system of economic imperialism which embodied none of the principles of free trade or fair trade.

Britain's first probe into the Americas came in 1608, when Captain John Smith and a crew of perhaps a dozen, with an herb doctor aboard, explored the Chesapeake Bay. In another quarter-century, settlers established Maryland's first colony in what is now St. Mary's County.

Davey Jones was among the first settlers to drift north; in 1661, he opened a store in what is now the Old Town section of Baltimore. Others soon followed, and a smattering of small ports sprang up — Coles Harbor, where Harborplace now sits, and Joppa Town, the Baltimore County seat on the Susquehanna River.

These five infant ports — Baltimore Town, Coles Harbor, Joppa Town, Whetstone Point and Humphrey's Creek — loosely strung like beads along the basin rim where the Patapsco makes land, would eventually meld into the Port of Baltimore.

Colonial Marylanders called it "sotte weed." We call it tobacco. These barrels full of tobacco are being loaded for shipping to Switzerland in 1947.

The kings of the Colonial economy were tobacco planters, whose wealth dwarfed the resources of early Baltimore Town. The planters developed Maryland's first maritime chains: small canoe-shaped sailboats sliced through the Patapsco's tributaries to dock at planters' wharves and load cured tobacco leaf, which was transported to ships in giant barrels called hogsheads sometimes rolled or horse-pulled to what is now Calvert Street — then the only road leading to the marshy expanse of Baltimore's harbor area, where wetlands extended west to what is now Charles Street and just north of Lombard to Water Street.

The English-born planters, who had seen the economic benefits of trade first-hand, spoke the language of maritime commerce. Since local consumption of any product was naturally limited, the key to greater profitability was the export or sale of tobacco to customers in distant markets. Of course, getting it there was another problem. Overland travel was dicey at best, always tedious and time-consuming. Water was shorter and surer; ships provided ready access to world markets, and had the added benefit of ample capacity.

And with their merchant mentality, the planters knew they needed to spend money to make money, so they invested in harbor development and shipyards, and also leaned on legislators for better roads to improve deliveries to waiting ships — a set of changes which improved the region's general business climate and encouraged fresh enterprise.

The planters' return on investment was substantial; Maryland's exports of "sotte weed" climbed from 30 million pounds in the 1720s to 100 million pounds in the 1770s. Emboldened by the dynamics of maritime trade, Marylanders began diversifying into other areas of agricultural production, and openly debated the merits of making a clean break from Britain, which perpetuated America's economic dependence by controlling the terms of Colonial trade.

On the Bay, boat traffic and commerce were picking up: Cargoes were transported in skiffs, flat-bottomed barges, canoes and larger vessels like a shallop — the open 30-footer John Smith used to explore the Bay — and a pinnace like the *Dove*, from which the very first English settlers disembarked onto the western shore of the Delmarva Peninsula.

The clock was ticking down on Colonial Maryland's deep sleep. Already, developments were afoot that would revolutionize the state of the economy and the state of the nation, and propel the Port of Baltimore to global pre-eminence. Scattered amidst tobacco warehouses in the Patapsco River Valley, the means of transitioning from an agricultural to an industrial economy — and the underpinnings of a diversified economic base — had been set in motion.

Baltimore's shipwrights, using the Chesapeake as a proving ground to test their designs, began developing a distinct style of boat built for speed and maneuverability, single-masted sloops and two-masted schooners which shook off pirates and French privateers who stalked them during trade expeditions to West Indies islands.

In a sense, much of the heavy lifting for Baltimore's growth was performed 35 million years earlier, give or take, when an extraterrestrial body (no one knows quite what, since it was vaporized) slammed into the mid-Atlantic coast at blinding speed and formed a crater, which became the Chesapeake.

A map from 1780 reveals the breadth of the Bay's reach into Maryland. Baltimore Harbor rests at the top of the Patapsco River shown in the upper-middle portion of the map beside the "A" in Maryland.

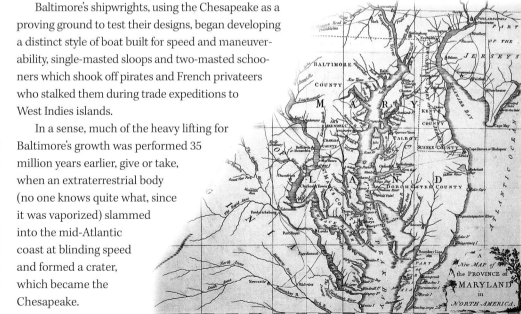

9

The resulting geography, and the Port's position relative to the Patapsco River Valley, the Bay and America's Midwest, laid the foundation for Baltimore's port to emerge as a commercial transportation hub.

There's a divide in Maryland's broad, brackish seam: the fabled "Land of Pleasant Living," sometimes called the world's best fishing hole, commands the Chesapeake to the south, while to the north the Port, in concert with Baltimore's adjoining downtown business district, occupies the business end.

The Port, with its ready access to sea lanes, was also adjacent to rich wheat and corn fields of northern Maryland and southern Pennsylvania, as well as the "fall line," where rivers like the Patapsco, Gwynns Falls and Jones Falls provide a natural means to power mill machinery in their descent from an interior plateau toward the tidewater.

Baltimore's two great rivals as the state's dominant maritime power mid-18th century were Fell's Point — whose status exceeded Baltimore's, owing to its superior harbor and growing notoriety in Colonial circles as the place to go to have a ship built — and Annapolis, where leading Maryland families like the Carrolls and Dulaneys entertained in their elegant Georgian town houses; like other members of Maryland's privileged class, their wealth and prominence principally emanated from the Port.

Overreliance on a single, seasonal agricultural crop like tobacco is the enemy of sustained economic growth: After Captain John Smith sailed up into the Bay, he named it River Bolus because the riverbanks emitted a hue which reminded him of a red resin called bole armoniack used in cosmetics, a coloring that actually emanated from plentiful iron ore deposits speckling the region. Principio Company, on the Gunpowder River in Cecil County, began producing iron in 1715. Nottingham Ironworks and Baltimore Ironworks soon followed, forming a robust manufacturing industry which used the Port as a gateway to ship tons of iron across the Atlantic, sometimes in the form of ballast for departing British ships traveling "light" or without cargoes. Ballast stone, later used to build the celebrated white steps of Baltimore's row houses, came across from England.

Shipyard Snapshots

Baltimore always built ships with the very best of them — built and launched them, mended and refurbished them, and broke ships apart for scrap metal when their useful economic lives ended.

No one innovated better, or launched more new types of vessels, from wooden sailing ships that cut through waves like clouds to mammoth troop carriers rushed into production to protect the free world.

America doesn't make great ships anymore. That industry has moved offshore. So it's unlikely Baltimore will ever be surpassed as a shipbuilding giant.

Shipyards are labor-intensive. At their peak during World War II, the three shipyard industries — building, repair, demolition — employed

Key to Baltimore's reputation as America's shipbuilding hub, the workers at Bethlehem Steel's Fairfield yard were a proud lot, especially when witnessing the launch of ships such as the Charles Carroll, below right, in 1943.

80,000 area residents; about 300 jobs remain today.

Boston Metals Company and Patapsco Scrap Company scrapped ships, reverse engineering in a sense — a teardown which mirrored shipbuilding processes. After interior fixtures were removed, the vessel was cut down, deck house by deck house, down to the keel plates.

Lesser-known Baltimore highlights include Bethlehem's construction of the world's first supertanker in 1948; "jumboizing" — welding in a new mid-section to increase capacity — a technique pioneered by Maryland Shipbuilding and Drydock Company; Sparrows Point's 1905 construction of the floating drydock Dewey, which was towed 13,000 miles to the Philippines, then described as the greatest feat in transoceanic navigation.

Left: A ship's propeller salvaged from shipbreaking at Sparrows Point Shipyard, which was sold at auction in 2004 to Barletta Willis Investments, LLC.
Center: Gas & Electric Tug No. 3 gets a boost at the railway at Smith Shipyard on Curtis Bay.
Right: Two harbor tugs rest in drydock at The General Ship Repair, the last shipyard on Key Highway.

River of Commerce

But it was grain, more than any other single bulk commodity, which built the Port of Baltimore. And it was along the Patapsco River Valley where Marylanders first mastered the industrial processes which transformed raw materials into exportable quantities of quality product — finished flour, that most basic of all foodstuffs.

The Patapsco, primarily perceived as a shipping channel to transport tobacco, instead emerged as a river of commerce, an industrial incubator for a host of nascent business operations which also seeded the birth of numerous mill towns, providing the Port with both investment capital and human capital — a foundation to sustain the era of heady, high-growth days awaiting Maryland.

The influx of Pennsylvania-German farmers into Maryland during the mid-1700s brought the three Ellicott brothers into the Patapsco Valley, where they developed the largest grain mill in Colonial America, the very model of industrial success others would emulate.

Word of their success attracted the attention of Oliver Evans, who only dropped by to interest the Ellicotts in steam power, but stuck around to become a maestro of Maryland's grain industry, encapsulating his state-of-the-art milling technology in the 1795 publication of "Young Mill-Wright and Miller's Guide," which went through 14 editions.

For the Ellicotts, one thing led to another. With the profits from their flour operations, they built copper and woolen mills, which in turn spun off a network of stores, shops, schools and churches, and jobs for clerks, millers, coopers, blacksmiths, wheelwrights and millwrights — the makings of Ellicott City. Other mill towns and

Facing page: The sun sets behind the Locust Point grain pier, the last working facility of its kind at the Port.

Above: Modern grain elevators at Canton evolved from early milling technology, such as the sketch at far left, by Oliver Evans.

Left: Andrew Ellicott helped develop what was once North America's largest grain mill.

13

ironworks took hold along the Patapsco in Avalon, Orange Grove, Ilchester, Gray's, Oella, Granite and Daniels.

The Patapsco's saga intersects the Port's business at numerous points. The river valley was an incubator for Maryland's textile and paper industries. The Ellicotts were the first to attempt to dredge Baltimore's harbor with their "mud machine" — a horse-drawn drag with iron scoops. Valley merchants and bankers were among the first to give voice and funding for what seemed like a radical concept at the time — a railroad.

Still others gravitated toward maritime-related enterprises, like the McKim family, which owned the Hockley Flour Mills north of Elk Ridge, who later put their money into the construction of the *Ann McKim*, considered the ultimate Baltimore clipper. It was also the largest, 143 feet in length. The 1832 launch of the 500-ton vessel was a high-water mark for Baltimore shipbuilders. The McKims also founded Maryland Chemical Works in 1825 at the foot of Patterson's wharf in the Inner Harbor, answering a need for a domestic chemical supplier for Baltimore's plants and factories.

Right: The magnificent
Ann McKim, considered the
ultimate Baltimore clipper.
Far right: Ilchester, along the
Patapsco River, was one of
many mill towns that produced
iron, grain and textiles.

The evolution of Ellicott City previewed the torrid growth which lay ahead for Baltimore, where conditions were coalescing to prime the Port's pump. The textbook factors of production were falling into place: labor, capital goods such as machines, factories and infrastructure, and an entrepreneurial class for organization and risk-taking.

Grain soon would overtake tobacco as Baltimore's leading export. Few know the name of John Stevenson, but a cargo of flour this shipyard owner shipped to his native Ireland in 1750 proved instrumental in putting Baltimore on the world map. The flour, because it was pure and mold-resistant, was a resounding success in Ireland. More overseas orders soon followed. Stevenson's ambition was to establish the Port of Baltimore as *the* flour exporter of choice for foreign markets; many regard him as the maritime pioneer whose vision was responsible for the bulk cargo transactions for which the Port subsequently became famous.

Carved into the waterfront just downriver from Baltimore Town lay Fell's Point, whose cobble-stoned roadways and English street names still evoke a quality of other-worldliness.

Even after Baltimore annexed Fell's Point in 1773, the river rivals remained a world apart in a sense, separated more by their differences than real distance. Baltimore was but a backwater, with little to recommend it except a rudimentary port, while Fell's Point, with its natural deep-water port, dealt in fast ships and fast times. If relatively little is known about Baltimore or its port before the Revolutionary War era, it's because there was little worth knowing.

But that would change; Baltimore's time was coming. Between 1752 and 1774, its housing stock increased from 24 to 564. Baltimore became the county seat in 1768, taking the weighty functions of local government — courts, jails and land records

— from Joppa Town. Cottage industry was complimented by new, heavier industry, such as a clayworks supplying building brick for a growing city. The quality and fine, natural color of Baltimore brick made it highly desirable; as an export, it was said to gild the front of opulent homes in Philadelphia, New York and Boston.

The fit between land and water in the port area was improved, expediting the critical commercial function of transporting goods between ship and shore. Port activity increased in lockstep with growing domestic demand; America was a growing nation.

Ships anchored in the harbor served as floating stores whose wares were advertised by word-of-mouth ashore to the man on the street — innkeepers, sail-makers, tailors, shoemakers, bricklayers, schoolmasters, hatters, teamsters, bakers, blacksmiths, clerks, barrel-makers, barbers, millers, stevedores and ship carpenters.

Above: The Washington Flour mill in Ellicott City still churns out flour and cake mixes.

Below: Baltimore's clayworks supplied building bricks for a city on the move. Due to its quality and color, Baltimore brick was in demand for the facades of many elegant East Coast mansions.

Patriotism Proves Profitable

Baltimore had arrived at its tipping point; the ingredients for economic growth were assembled. All that was needed was a catalyst, a pull on the trigger that the opening shots of America's Revolutionary War provided.

Any show of force against the British navy would have to be shouldered by the men with the money, America's merchant princes. Syndicates of Baltimore businessmen financed the construction of 250 armed ships called privateers. Fast, predatory and privately owned privateers carried "letters of marque and reprisal," papers signed by government officials authorizing the vessels to conduct military operations on behalf of the United States, including the capture of enemy merchant ships. Privateers worked on a "no prey, no pay" basis; the spoils of war were split among ship owners, captain and crew.

Baltimore delivered the first two seagoing vessels to America's infant navy, the *Wasp* and the *Hornet*, cruisers whose very names suggest the sting-and-disable strategy used to deflate the firepower of larger British frigates. The first U.S. frigate, the 28-gun *Virginia*, was built in Fell's Point.

Patriotism proved profitable for the Port. For starters, it eliminated, in word if not deed, restrictions Britain had imposed on Colonial maritime commerce — although Britain continued to menace sea lanes in the North Atlantic, the West Indies and elsewhere, and commandeered Baltimore ships until 1815.

Secondly, because the British never blockaded the Port, much of the Annapolis trade was permanently diverted into Baltimore, clearing the way for Baltimore to become Maryland's pre-eminent maritime center. Thirdly, Baltimore's reputation as a shipbuilding center was enhanced by the performance of its ships and sailors, which in turn generated new business orders. Lastly, maritime industries which sprang up during the war — such as Baltimore's first rope walk in Fell's Point, a distinctively long and slender building used to manually twist and bind separate strands to create rope for rigging for privateers — were up and running. Removal of Colonial restrictions on manufacturing was good news for Maryland industry, which diversified to expand the Port's export base.

Imports increased, too; coffee and tea were stocked at the Lexington Market, which opened in 1782, soon followed by the Center Market at Baltimore and Harrison streets, popularly called Marsh's Market because it was built on filled-in wetland.

Facing page: Cocoa, used in products from cosmetics to candy, is among the international cargoes handled by the Port. Above: Baltimoreans shopped for produce at Lexington Market in the early 20th century, top, as well as the early 21st century, middle, and made Center Market, bottom, a stop for fresh goods.

A visual sweep of the harbor area from atop Federal Hill after the war gave early evidence that the multiplier effect of maritime commerce — its ability to multiply investment dollars by spinning off new business from other sectors linked into the maritime chain — had taken firm hold on Baltimore's economy.

Below was the Port's first shipyard, at the foot of Federal Hill, opened in 1773 by Thomas Morgan, and a groundswell of other start-ups, clusters of small shipyards ringed by woodworks and metal works. Before too long, engine shops, breweries, small iron and steel mills, fertilizer and chemical plants, and ice storage houses would dot the shoreline.

Toward the Inner Harbor area were wharves and markets, wholesalers and shippers, while Fell's Point's waterfront was a forest of masts and canvas. Further south downriver in Canton the *Constellation*, America's first frigate, was launched from David Stodder's Boston Street shipyard on Harris Creek in 1797.

In 1783, nine warders — the equivalent of present-day port commissioners — were authorized to survey and chart the basin, harbor and Patapsco River, clear and measure the main channel, and charge all vessels using it.

That same year, work was completed on a block-long canal extending from the harbor up to Water Street. The canal area — a base of operations for Captain John Daniel Daniels' privateers — was called Cheapside, a name taken from a disreputable dockside in London. Wharf timbers from the canal, which was earthed over in 1814 to extend Pratt Street across the Port's northern boundary, were unearthed during the 1984 construction of The Gallery opposite Harborplace.

Baltimore's population doubled during the 1790s. Baltimore Town became Baltimore City in 1797; formalities were delayed until the General Assembly agreed to demands from Fell's Pointers to be exempted from paying taxes to deepen the harbor.

Growing maritime trade, and increasingly complex commercial transactions, necessitated the need for more sophisticated financial services. State legislators authorized the establishment of the Bank of Maryland in 1790, and in 1792 the Baltimore branch of the Bank of the United States opened for business. Banks stimulated the regional economy by establishing paper money as a medium of exchange, and increased available credit. Word of Baltimore's ascendancy was spread on the pages of its six newspapers. The first federal census in 1790 reported that Baltimore Town was America's fifth most populous urban area with 13,503 people.

East met west in Colonial America the day Captain John O'Donnell sailed into Baltimore's harbor in 1785 aboard his merchant frigate, the *Pallas*. Among his crew of Moors and Malays were several thought to be the first Chinese to set foot in America. His exquisite cargo of rare teas, silks, satins and china set tongues wagging, including that of George Washington, who inquired about their price. O'Donnell bought nearly 2,000 acres of waterfront property east of Fell's Point, built a lavish Oriental-styled home, and named his estate Canton, after the port city in south China whose freewheeling trade had already made him a rich man. His heirs created the Canton Company, which became integral in Baltimore's maritime and industrial scheme of things.

Above: A view from Federal Hill circa 1831 shows the harbor skyline. Some early harbor buildings are still standing.

Facing page: The *Constellation*, America's first frigate, leaves the harbor to call at the Naval Academy in Annapolis.

Baltimore, Inc.

The Port's outbound trade — whose value climbed from $2,027,000 in 1790 to $16,610,000 in 1799 — was the only thing rising faster than the number of Baltimore-area incorporations. Cargoes spilled out of more than 170 warehouses around the Port; most contained exports to be shipped out, but there also were incoming finished imports, life's finer things like choice bed linens for Baltimore's emerging upscale market.

Baltimore and its port were both moving up in the rankings: By the turn of the century, the commercial value of the Port's cargoes was third-highest nationally, and Baltimore was America's third biggest city with 26,524 residents.

The Port's East Coast trade now roamed between Rhode Island and South Carolina, and from London to Lisbon abroad, with stops in China, the Caribbean and the Canary Islands. Rumblings from the business community that congestion would limit the Port's growth pushed the issue to the top of Baltimore's agenda. Wharves were extended with the help of new machinery capable of driving piles to accommodate the Port's burgeoning trade, and channels were dredged regularly, as Baltimore's development advanced block by block across the downtown marshland, and pier by pier along the waterfront.

By the early 1800s, just several decades removed from the time when a solitary finger pier was all that met the eye, the Port's creep began to command a greater share of Baltimore Town's shoreline, presaging its eventual need to push downriver.

The magnitude of the modern-day Port of Baltimore, extending over a 40-square-mile area of the Patapsco River waterfront, exceeds the easy grasp of casual observers. But inadequate space for maritime operations, which concerned Baltimoreans two centuries ago, continues to vex the waterfront community today.

Ports occupy America's choice coastal real estate, parcels hotly coveted for residential development and recreation. Ports typically are also in heavily-congested urban areas, boxed-in by extensive infrastructure such as railroads, industrial sites and power plants — a tight fit leaving little room to expand.

The heavy increase in foreign trade volume, projected to double within 10 years, has exceeded already the capacity of many major U.S. ports, which sometimes must turn away business, or transport overflow goods many miles away for temporary keeping, increasing operating costs and sending business into the arms of their competitors.

Facing page: The view from the HarborView tower, which was built on the site of the graving dock of the Bethlehem Steel Key Highway repair yard. Top: Cargo is unloaded at Canton in 1935 from a sailing ship. Above: Forest products, a key Port commodity, await shipment at BalTerm's South Locust Point terminal.

Captains of Industry

The Port's enriched flows of waterfront commerce generated a brisk business for protecting maritime valuables; in 1798 alone, Fell's Point's export cargoes exceeded $121 million. Between 1787 and 1815, 10 insurance companies — five specializing in marine risks — were started in Baltimore. The business of insuring cargoes provided an injection of capital into Baltimore — an example of maritime's indirect economic stimulus.

And as the value of the Port's commercial flows increased, so did recognition that greater value lay in the Port's uniquely amphibious position, with one foot further inland than its East Coast competitors, and the other foot planted in the sea lanes leading outward to world markets. Baltimore's port has variously been called the most western of all Eastern seaports, the most southern of the Northern ports, or the most northern of all Southern ports. Baltimore's proximity to choice markets was a trump card played time and again against rival ports.

If there was ever a time when the Port's commercial power and shipbuilding prowess were both running fully flat-out, it was during the first half of the 19th century — a period not coincidentally regarded as Baltimore's Golden Age.

Baltimore's burst to glory was driven by the synchronicity between the Port and Maryland's business and civic machinery, orchestrated by captains of industry like Alexander Brown.

In 1811, a little more than a decade after he arrived from Ireland, Brown opened the nation's first investment bank at 135 East Baltimore Street. By the 1820s, his firm was a powerful force in international trade and finance. Brown, like other merchants, made his first fortune in trade — in his case, Irish linens — and subsequently widened his net to include shipping. By 1825, he controlled a fleet of 11 vessels.

Brown's trajectory typifies others who left their names on Baltimore's better-known institutions that still endure since being established during the latter part of the 19th century; in 1893, Baltimore reportedly had more millionaire philanthropists than any other American city.

Enoch Pratt, who bequeathed funds for Baltimore's public library system, made his money through trade, shipping and investing in businesses spun off by the Port's commercial flows — finance,

Many of Baltimore's early movers and shakers sailed the path to wealth on investments in Port-related industries. Above, from left, Alexander Brown founded the nation's first investment bank, which was located on East Baltimore Street; philanthropist Enoch Pratt lent his name and fortune to the city's public library.

insurance and transportation. Johns Hopkins, who put his name on Baltimore's world-class hospital system and university, also grew rich through assorted maritime-related investments. The Walters and Peabody families, benefactors of two beacons of Baltimore's high culture — the midtown museum and musical conservatory — sailed similar paths to great wealth.

Of course, the impact of merchants enriched by trade also reverberated throughout Maryland's social life. Baltimore was still in its formative stage, with little sense of identity, enviously eyeing its more cosmopolitan neighbors like Philadelphia and New York to the north. The city's captains of industry, if only by default, were the role models and arbiters of taste for many upwardly mobile Baltimoreans.

The Port's footprint extends further to the state's transportation network. The first Colonial roads were nothing more than animal paths and routes worn bare by the foot traffic of Native Americans. Long before any white man ever laid eyes on the prize real estate at the northern reaches of the Patapsco River, the Nanticoke, Piscataway and Susquehannock tribes were plying the estuary's brackish waters for food. Indians named the Port's essential waterways: "Patapsco," which first appears on 1655 land grants, is said to refer to a bevy of sandstone rocks rising 20 feet above the surface off Rock Creek near the river's mouth. "Chesapeake," ascribed to the Algonquin tribe, means "great shellfish water."

Time always has been of the essence in maritime trade, since ships turn no profit dockside. Land arteries were the weak link in Colonial Maryland's maritime chain; many shippers died a slow death awaiting cargoes mired in muddy, narrow pathways.

As traffic thickened on byways into Baltimore, particularly from the state's western frontier area, tolls were exacted to develop Maryland's transportation infrastructure. But as the business community kept agitating to bring Maryland's land transport up to par with ocean transport, legislators acted: by 1809, three great toll roads or turnpikes — Frederick, York and Reisterstown — had been built. Freight now could be hauled year-round. Falls Road, Harford Road, Washington Road and a road to Havre de Grace soon followed.

Baltimore Clippers

After a brief interlude between wars with Britain, Baltimore's maritime community proved even more decisive during the War of 1812.

With America again at war, the Port's shipyards moved into full production. Baltimore commissioned more privateers than any other American seaport, launching about 120 ships which captured more than 500 British sloops. The *Chasseur*, built in Fell's Point, captured 11 vessels on her first trans-Atlantic crossing; during her second, the *Chasseur* outdid that by single-handedly beleaguering shipping traffic up and down the entire English coast to become hailed as the "Pride of Baltimore" upon her return.

Still licking the wounds Baltimore's fleet inflicted during the Revolution, British soldiers torched Washington, D.C., in August 1814 and turned north, seeking revenge on Baltimore's "nest of pirates." Chains were stretched across the water from Fort McHenry to Lazaretto Point, attached to a row of scuttled schooners, to prevent the greatest invasion fleet ever in American waters from entering Baltimore's harbor.

Francis Scott Key found himself in the wrong place at the right time: detained aboard a ship during the British bombardment of Fort McHenry, he jotted down lyrics on the back of a letter which became the story line for America's national anthem — "The Star-Spangled Banner."

Of all the watercraft produced by Chesapeake Bay shipbuilders, none is more famous than the "Baltimore Clipper," smallish schooners whose maneuverability and terrific speed — twice that of other merchant ships — made them ideal for warfare and interdiction. With their V-shaped hulls and tall masts to support relatively large sails, these ocean antelopes could sail close to or "clip" the wind. Since they sacrificed cargo space for speed, Baltimore Clippers were best-suited for low-volume, high-profit commercial ventures such as spice, tea and mail deliveries.

Disposing of the spoils of war required legitimate merchant channels, which boosted Baltimore's economy. Fell's Point became home to more ship captains and owners, whose upscale residences featured wallpaper, interior and exterior trim, even chair rails. Samuel Kirk became America's most celebrated early 19th-century silversmith; his ornate repousse silverware decorated all the best tables. Kirk, like others whose business lived and died on the strength of imports and exports, set up shop hard by the harbor at Market (later Baltimore) Street. Samuel Kirk and Sons was later bought by the company that neighboring competitor Charles Stieff had founded in 1892.

Facing page: Fort McHenry, the birthplace of the national anthem. Above, left: Clipper ships also delivered cargo, including cigars. Above, center: An historic sketch from 1799 shows the *Constellation* and *L'Insurgente* battling. Above, right: Fort McHenry protected Baltimore Harbor during the War of 1812.

Bigger & Better

Refinements, meanwhile, were under way on a technology that imposed a sea change on the existing model of maritime commerce. Wind power was replaced by the mechanical force of steam power, which ramped up the maritime chain's capabilities and increased the volume of industrial outputs for ports to handle.

The first steamboats appeared in Baltimore's harbor in 1813. Now, steam-powered vessels could navigate the Chesapeake at regularly scheduled times, strengthening Baltimore's mastery as the Bay's dominant port and increasing commerce on both sides of the Chesapeake.

Depending on the need, steamers, which resembled a cross between a barge and a small ocean liner, provided basic cargo transportation or luxury accommodations for overnight cruises. Either way, they were the Port's economic lifeline until rendered obsolete by subsequent transportation developments like the interstate highway system and Bay Bridge. The Baltimore Steam Packet Line, affectionately called the Old Bay Line, founded in 1840 with Enoch Pratt as the lead investor, was the oldest existing

steamship line in the United States when it finally ended its Norfolk run in 1962.

The Industrial Revolution had other implications for shipping. Greater mechanical speed and reliability meant that larger batches of manufactured products could be made in less time, which created demand for more ships to move product to market, and more roads. Baltimore's flour exporters were among the first merchants to use steam to power milling operations dockside and reduce transportation costs; by the late 1820s, Baltimore became the world's biggest flour market.

Soon, the Port's pace would really quicken: Up in New York, they were digging a great ditch — more than 350 miles long — to allow boats to travel from Lake Erie to the Hudson River, giving the rival New Yorkers access to Baltimore's highly profitable Midwest markets. And if that wasn't bad enough, another waterway, the C&O Canal, threatened to provide other ports with Midwest access via the Potomac River.

But steam-engine technology also had been applied to land travel. The *Tom Thumb*, America's first steam-powered locomotive or "steam carriage" as it was billed — one-horsepower engine and all — was built in Baltimore in 1830 by Peter Cooper. Alarmed by the threat posed by canals, Cooper only wanted to hedge his investment in Canton real estate. His was the tiny steam-powered engine which could and did: the *Tom Thumb* proved the feasibility of rail travel when it made a round trip to Ellicott City.

In 1827, Maryland's legislators, driven by fears Baltimore's port would lose its choice Midwest markets, chartered the Baltimore and Ohio Railroad — the first step toward the development of an overland transportation network which, in tandem with steam power, transformed the Port's commerce and American industry.

At the time, canals were considered the epitome of overland transportation; railroads represented a giant technological leap of faith.

The concept of adapting an apparatus used in mines to long-distance transport seemed far-fetched to many. But merchants in the Patapsco River Valley supported the idea and signed on as investors, hoping to minimize their transport costs; the B&O's first few miles of track were laid down in their valley. As the century progressed, Maryland's assorted ship, canal and rail initiatives were the underpinnings of much of the state's economic progress, enabling metropolitan Baltimore to evolve into a gateway for national and international transport.

Facing page: Steam engine technology revolutionized freight and passenger service. Light Street docks teemed with draymen, drivers of carts without fixed sides. Peter Cooper, inset, developed the first locomotive, the *Tom Thumb*, shown in a sketch, far left. Above and left: Steamboats like the *Emma Giles* carried passengers to vacation spots.

Changing of the Guard

On July 4, 1828, Charles Carroll of Carrollton turned the first spade of earth for the ceremonial laying of the cornerstone at B&O's Mt. Clare headquarters in West Baltimore.

The moment was rich in symbolism.

When Carroll died, he was the richest man in America and the last surviving signer of the Declaration of Independence. Carroll was a planter. John Work Garrett, who would become B&O president, was an industrialist. The guard had changed.

Carroll's fortune had funded Baltimore's great Colonial houses — Mt. Clare and Homewood House. Garrett would go a step better and build Evergreen House, touching off another round of domicile development among Baltimore's upper crust.

Garrett, although nominally a railroad man, arguably exerted a greater influence over the fortunes of the Port of Baltimore than any other single individual. Until his death in 1884, he was considered the most powerful person in the state.

Then, as now, Baltimore's port and railroads form a true symbiotic relationship — both benefit from the other's presence and good health.

Determined to fully leverage his most valuable asset, Garrett opened up new markets for the Port by extending rail lines westward, and built a marine terminal at Locust Point where cargoes could be transferred directly between trains and ships without intermediary handling — an innovation which the rest of the industry would follow. Garrett later hedged his bet by buying a fleet of steamships; his vessels were the only operating U.S.-flag ships engaged in ocean trade after the Civil War.

Locust Point marks the spot where visitors to today's Inner Harbor see the 120-by-70-foot Domino Sugar sign, a landmark claimed to be America's second-largest neon construction east of

Facing page: The CSX railyard at Locust Point. Above: Two financiers — Charles Carroll of Carrollton, upper left, and John Work Garrett, left — were founders of the B&O Railroad. Carroll was reputedly America's richest man when he died and Garrett was considered one of Maryland's most powerful men. Garrett expanded the railroad to link the Port to lucrative Midwest markets and brought railcars directly to the piers.

Las Vegas. Unseen by most outside Maryland's maritime community — sitting west of Fort McHenry — is Locust Point's marine terminal, one of the largest sea and rail complexes ever built, a grain and coal colossus instrumental in putting Baltimore on the world map.

Garrett's empire-building strategy — driven by his determination to maximize the Port's yield — had a profound impact on Maryland's economy.

First there was the rolling stock: Just between 1848 and 1851, Mt. Clare turned out 190 locomotives alone. Hundreds of railroad bridges needed to be built; Wendel Bollman, after working as an engineer for B&O, developed America's first cast-iron bridge. Shops, offices, rail stations and operational buildings were constructed, which necessitated street improvements and more employee housing. Finally, supplier and support industries were also required. All of this activity created demand for brick and iron, for engineers and architects, and general labor.

The B&O was not the only game in town. At the same time the Western Maryland was developing, the Northern Central Railroad, controlled by the Pennsylvania Railroad, also began, while the Canton Company, through Alexander Brown and Co., had built the Union Railroad.

Of course, this competitive frenzy of railroad-building was driven by the presence and commercial appeal of the Port, and the inevitable sequel was the railroads' subsequent attempts to tighten their grip on Baltimore's maritime commerce through increased investment and construction of massive marine terminals, which provided thousands of new jobs and intensified the Port's multiplier effect on Maryland's economy.

The Port's rail rivalry had indirect benefits, opening up places such as Ocean City in Worcester County on the Eastern Shore. For years, its trickle of visitors had to hire small boats to cross Sinepuxent Bay until it was bridged by a rail trestle in 1876. By 1891, Baltimoreans could reach the resort just six hours after boarding a departing steamer at Light Street.

The Port acquired a second access route to international sea lanes with the completion of the 14-mile Chesapeake and Delaware Canal in 1829, a real time-saver for deepwater North Atlantic traffic or northern East Coast ports.

Above: A ship navigates the Chesapeake and Delaware Canal, trailed by an oil barge under tow. The canal connects the Port of Baltimore with Philadelphia's oil refineries and cargo facilities.
Left: Two American-flag steamships are loaded with grain in 1929 at the Western Maryland Railroad pier at Port Covington.

By 1830, Baltimore was the second-largest American city, with 80,620 people. Arunah S. Abell began publishing *The Sun* in 1837, spreading the good word about Maryland's economic muscle: Baltimore's port had surpassed Philadelphia to become second only to New York on the East Coast. Coal and grain were the leading exports, but as coffee imports kept climbing, new coffee warehouses crowded the Thames Street corridor in Fell's Point. Baltimore was full of (coffee) beans; Belt's Wharf began as a terminal for the coffee fleet of C. Morton Stewart, whose clipper *Josephine* set a record for the fastest passage from Rio de Janeiro, 22 days. Today, Belt's Corporation has evolved into a leading mid-Atlantic provider of distribution services.

From the observatory tower atop Federal Hill, telescopes peered over the lower Patapsco 60 miles downriver. When an incoming vessel was recognized, its owner's flag was hoisted from the tower to notify Baltimore merchants the ship had arrived safely. In waterfront neighborhoods like Fell's Point, owners also flew their flags outside their homes.

The C&O Canal finally reached Cumberland in 1850; cargoes now could be moved to and from southern states and heavily-populated Midwestern locations. More freight called for more railroads. In 1852, the predecessor of the Western Maryland Railroad — the Baltimore, Carroll and Frederick — was chartered.

The B&O's sweeping orbit provided Baltimore with architectural prestige: In 1850, Bartlett, Hayward & Company moved next door to B&O's shops and began producing cast-iron architectural components, which led to the 1851 construction of the Sun Iron Building at Baltimore and South streets, the forerunner of the modern skyscraper, the first building in America with a cast-iron facade and iron post-and-beam frame. Within 18 months, 22 new downtown Baltimore buildings incorporated cast iron in their construction; cities worldwide took notice of the new technology.

The Association of Maryland Pilots was organized in Duda's Tavern in Fell's Point in 1852. In the early days, pilots would hover in their boats at the mouth of the Chesapeake awaiting incoming vessels; when a sail was sighted on the horizon, they would all race toward it, with the winning boat being the first to throw a line to the ship. The select members of the oldest pilots' association in the United States still board incoming ships at Cape Henry by scurrying onboard via a Jacob's ladder thrown over the side to become temporary master for the 150-mile run upriver. Bay pilots are tasked with negotiating the usual local

Above: Immigrants line up on Wolfe Street, waiting for transportation to the country for berry picking. Inset: Bartlett, Hayward & Co. pioneered the modern skyscraper and helped make Baltimore's architectural innovations the envy of the world.

hazards — strong winds, changing channel depths, rain and snow, and the unexpected moves of rookie boaters.

Incoming waves of immigrants — first primarily from southern Europe, and then eastern Europe — supplied manpower for Baltimore's multitude of maritime-related enterprises. The newcomers disembarked in Locust Point, Fell's Point and Canton, greeted on their arrival by the stars and stripes waving over Fort McHenry.

Between the mid-1830s and the onset of the Civil War, Baltimore doubled its population, workforce, housing stock, street mileage and developed area. City boundaries were extended northward to North Avenue, south to Fort McHenry and east to Ellwood Street, as Baltimore grew from three to 10 square miles.

By 1850, Baltimore's population had rocketed to 169,054. Only New York City was larger.

And there was no slack in Port traffic; a new Custom House was built to keep pace with its growing commerce. Long Dock along Pratt Street was crowded with watercraft selling melons, tomatoes and potatoes. More steamboat lines were added to meet the demand for foreign and domestic trade, but the big news in shipbuilding circles was the 1855 launch of the *Mary Whitridge*, the fastest clipper ever built, from the Fell's Point yard of Hunt and Wagner. On her maiden voyage, she set a sail speed record which still stands, charging from the Chesapeake's mouth to the English Channel in 12 days, 7 hours.

Gold had been discovered in California. New orders poured into the Port's shipyards for fast ships, Baltimore Clippers, the only vessels capable of making the turn around the treacherous horn of South America and reaching the West Coast in under 100 days.

Demand for new ships occupied much of the waterfront's business; more than 90 percent of all America's imports and exports were then transported on U.S.-flag ships, so shipbuilding boomed. Ross Winans launched his famous "cigar ship" into the Patapsco's middle branch in 1858. Long, round and very thin, it was propelled by an iron wheel with flanges that encircled the vessel at mid-ships.

Shipyard Saga

A seminal figure in America's 19th-century abolitionist movement, Frederick Douglass was born into slavery on Maryland's Eastern Shore. During the mid-1830s, Douglass found work at Baltimore shipyards as a caulker, stuffing a ropelike material called 'oakum" — which had been soaked in tar — between wooden planks to make ships watertight.

Disguised as a sailor, Douglass escaped Baltimore in 1838 and settled in Europe, where his skill as an orator enabled him to raise money to buy his freedom. Returning to America, he befriended Abraham Lincoln, inspiring his Emancipation Proclamation.

Isaac Myers, "born free" in Baltimore in 1835, soon became a master ship caulker supervising caulking on clipper ships. In 1865, as racial tensions flared, shipyard owners phased out black labor. Led by Myers, black workers organized a joint stock company to raise funds to start their own shipyard; Douglass was an early stockholder.

In 1868, the Chesapeake Marine Railway and Dry Dock Company in Fell's Point turned a tidy profit as America's first black-operated shipyard, hiring regardless of race. Myers went on to become a national labor leader.

Above: Frederick Douglass. Left: Founded in 1852, the Association of Maryland Pilots is the oldest such organization in America. Today's pilots still access moving ships via the Jacob's ladder from a launch.

The March of Industry

Federal Hill made a fine Union fort during America's Civil War. Cannon batteries guarded the waterfront area, which had strategic value to the Union as a seaport and rail link between Washington and northern East Coast cities.

With the Civil War over and the economy in tatters, Maryland's leaders looked once again toward the Port for deliverance. The first order of business was to revitalize Baltimore's shipping industry and repair railroads damaged by Confederate raiders. The business community seized upon a southern strategy; efforts soon were under way to help rebuild the Confederacy and expand trade with South America, a source for the importation of sugar, and then Peruvian bird guano.

Baltimore became a world leader in manufacturing fertilizer, which was also in demand regionally to replenish soils depleted by decades of tobacco growing. By 1880, the city had 27 fertilizer factories. The Lazaretto Guano Works in Canton was an early producer. Lazaretto Point was also home to the harbor's most famous lighthouse; in 1916 it became the first such sentinel in

A ship off-loads raw sugar at the American Sugar Refining Company, manufacturer of Domino Sugar, an Inner Harbor landmark since 1921.

Cotton Duck

Above, left: Two skipjacks harvested oysters under sail in 1940. The vessel would transfer its catch to a buyboat. Above, right: Sailing vessels from skipjacks to schooners used heavy cotton duck to make sailcloth. Mills along the Jones Falls produced 80 percent of the world's cotton duck by 1880.

Maryland and Virginia to be electrified. Banking on the promise of the Port's increased trade, the region's first glass factory set up shop, followed by a paper box factory. In 1867, the first oil refinery began operations.

And with the Port in play to provide ready access to world markets, there was no stopping the march of industry, which diversified the statewide economy by taking fuller advantage of Maryland's natural resources.

The Port's first canning operations were established in the 1840s. The rotation of oysters in the winter, and fruits and vegetables in summer and fall, provided steady work for both canners and harvesters. Federal Hill, Canton and Fell's Point became home to innumerable canneries. Baltimore remained a global leader in canned food exports until the middle of the 20th century.

Cotton duck, a rugged fabric used for ships' sails, illustrates the interdependence between the Port and Maryland's economy. The state's textile industry dates from the 1808 opening of the Union Manufacturing Company's $1 million mill on Patapsco Falls, soon followed by the Washington Cotton Manufacturing Company and Powhatan Cotton Mills. Grist mills along the Jones Falls were converted into mechanized spinning and weaving plants in the early 1800s. By 1880, Baltimore produced 80 percent of the world's cotton duck, and until World War II, when Bethlehem Steel increased production, no Maryland industry employed more workers than did textiles.

The Port's competitive position took strength from two post-Civil War developments.

The first was the federally authorized, $400,000 dredging of the main Craighill access channel to a depth of 24 feet and a width of 250 feet to accommodate larger steamships bearing bigger cargoes. At about six million cubic yards, the sediment removed from the floor of Baltimore's harbor was twice the volume of Egypt's Great Pyramid.

Sediment arouses strong sentiment on the waterfront. Back in Baltimore's dark ages, a navigable harbor was so vital that town officials deemed it a crime to throw dirt or sand into the Patapsco, punishable by a fine of five British pounds — a whopping one month's salary in the early 18th century. The ongoing need for harbor dredging, as well as control over the placement of dredged material, remain problematic issues which still vex Maryland's maritime community in the early 21st century, and will be closely monitored.

The second key development, a "differential" imposed by Interstate Commerce Commission regulators on railroad companies, instituted a freight system in which the cost of moving goods was made proportional to the overland distance the goods moved: For a Chicago merchant, it suddenly became cheaper to ship goods through Baltimore's port as opposed to New York, reflecting the fact that Baltimore is 90 miles closer to Chicago.

The differential — whose groundwork was laid down by John Work Garrett and Enoch Pratt, a major investor in the B&O until his death in 1873 — helped equalize the natural gifts enjoyed by New York's port, whose vast harbor adjacent to the sea, the Hudson River and an extensive railroad network was a strategic advantage over rival ports.

Canton was emerging as the Port's heavy industrial arm. O'Donnell's 3,000-acre estate, which included all the waterfront property from Fell's Point to Lazaretto Point opposite Fort McHenry, was developed piecemeal by industries enticed by the prospects of partnering with some aspect of the Port's lines of business.

Canton's commercial orientation was distinctly maritime — refineries and smelters turning out copper products that resist the corrosive effects of salt water, and iron mills and foundries. The Baltimore Copper Company was among the first to locate there; with Enoch Pratt and Johns Hopkins on board as lead investors,

it was America's largest copper refinery before being recast as American Smelting and Refining Company. Most ships then manufactured in America were sheathed in copper, which accounts for the longevity of the *Constellation* in today's Inner Harbor. In 1848, the Booz Shipyard was established on Harris Creek at the foot of Kenwood Avenue.

Horace Abbott's Canton Iron Works (first started by Peter Cooper), capable of manufacturing the largest rolled plate in the United States by 1850, built armor plates for the first iron battleship, the *Monitor*. The Patapsco Bridge & Iron Works gained a national reputation for its engineering feats, and built many of the bridges spanning the Jones Falls.

Railroad and steamboat connections to the Port profited watermen and helped open up Chestertown, Centreville, Oxford, Cambridge, Crisfield and Berlin on the Delmarva Peninsula by injecting commerce and capital into the regional economy.

The Canton Company completed the Canton Railroad in 1914, providing direct connections between industry and three major railroads: the Baltimore & Ohio, the Pennsylvania and the Western Maryland lines. Today, the Canton Railroad's brightly painted engines continue to provide short line service for CSX and Norfolk Southern.

City of Neighborhoods

Fell's Point, which rose on its deep-water allure, declined as a destination for oceanic trade after Garrett's 1867 agreement with the North German Lloyd Steamship line to begin regular steamship runs between Baltimore and Bremen. Since Fell's Point's wharves were too small to accommodate steamers, Garrett decided to develop a marine terminal at Locust Point across the river, constructing special facilities to handle grain and coal. The idea worked so well that the Pennsylvania Railroad soon duplicated it in Canton. Within a few years, Fell's Point's trade was confined to flour and coffee.

Coal was long one of the Port's bulk mainstays; much of it came from fields in Western Maryland, where production peaked at seven million tons in 1907. The long arm of the Port routinely has helped shape the economic development of regions throughout the state, but seldom as forcefully as in the Cumberland and Hagerstown areas, where railroads and coal mining sustained generations.

The invention of the sewing machine, coupled with Baltimore's superior regional transportation network, improved the city's grip on the garment market and kept the Port busy moving textiles. The advertising needs of Baltimore's clothing manufacturers employed hundreds. More than 100 packinghouses around the harbor in 1870 were needed to handle the prodigious output of Baltimore's canners, an export which in turn drove the manufacture of tin sheet and packing cases. When the B&O's tracks reached Chicago in 1875, a vast new market was laid open. Grain, coal and beef poured into the Port for export; Baltimore's customs revenues increased tenfold.

The J.S. Young Licorice Extract Company, America's first licorice candy maker, opened on Boston Street in 1869. Licorice root, imported from Middle Eastern nations, is in greatest demand by the tobacco and pharmaceutical industries; two days of factory output satisfied America's annual consumption of licorice-flavored candy.

By 1877, the value of the Port's foreign commerce was $62 million — a $17 million increase in five years. Imports overtook exports in 1883, with 795,524 tons versus 662,542 tons. The value of Baltimore's domestic trade was higher than foreign trade, and remained so until just before World War II.

Baltimore had, by the 1890s, emerged as a city of neighborhoods. Stable residential patterns created a diverse and interwoven metropolis that worked hard and worked together, a place where sons joined fathers on the same shop floor. Immigrants found work at shipyards, factories, canneries and packinghouses — enterprises which owed their existence to some manner of the Port's greater global presence.

Facing page: CNS handles six million tons of coal a year, processing from its state-of-the-art yard. Above, left: Millworkers were kept busy providing textiles for export after the invention of sewing machines. Above, right: C. Steinweg's terminal at North Locust Point handles a variety of commodities, including cocoa.

Baltimore is served by two Class I railroads, CSX and Norfolk Southern. CSX is the result of the consolidation of many of the lines that first served Baltimore — the Baltimore & Ohio, Chesapeake & Ohio and Western Maryland.

While John Work Garrett stood to gain the most from the rail differential, there was profit aplenty for Baltimore's railroads during the latter part of the 19th century.

It was the era when Baltimore finally gained entry into the uppermost echelon of great American cities, swept along by the Port's booming bulk trade which drew from — and economically contributed to — every corner of Maryland.

Railroads tied it all together, wheeling and dealing their way closer to the banks of the Patapsco until they eventually owned or controlled most of the Port's piers and waterfront facilities for both general and bulk cargoes — a situation existing in no major American port city, and one which returned to haunt Baltimore.

Federal Hill was steamship central. Charles Reeder's shop specialized in fabricating and installing engines, starting with Baltimore's first steamer, the paddle-wheeled *Chesapeake*. The Skinner yard built barks and brigs for the coffee trade. The Booz Brothers moved over from Canton in 1879; Redman and Vane specialized in repairing wooden ships. Half of Baltimore turned out in 1890 to watch the launching of the *Howard Cassard* — an odd duck named for a Baltimore lard mogul who financed the radically designed vessel, 222 feet long and only 16 feet wide. It was like trying to make a board float edgewise; unable to sit upright, the boat later was scrapped.

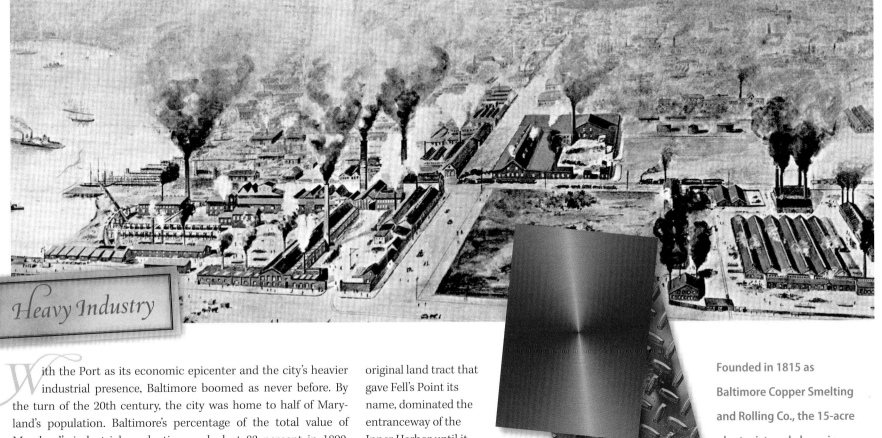

Heavy Industry

With the Port as its economic epicenter and the city's heavier industrial presence, Baltimore boomed as never before. By the turn of the 20th century, the city was home to half of Maryland's population. Baltimore's percentage of the total value of Maryland's industrial production peaked at 83 percent in 1890. New York, Philadelphia and Boston may have exuded more cosmopolitan appeal, but Baltimore bellowed with the commercial appeal of a workingman's town.

Baltimore's heavy industry was heavily invested in the region's human capital. Tens of thousands were hired by factories like Baltimore Smelting and Refining, Baltimore Drydock and Shipbuilding, Maryland Steel Company and the Fell's Point operations of Isaac Tyson, known as the "Chrome King of the World" until deposits of high-grade ore found abroad destroyed his monopoly. After Allied Chemical took over, the chrome plant, on the tip of William Fell's

original land tract that gave Fell's Point its name, dominated the entranceway of the Inner Harbor until it was demolished in the late 1980s.

America's first submarine, the *Argonaut*, 33 feet long and nine feet wide, was built in 1897 at the Columbian Iron Works, one of three ship repair yards with drydocks on Locust Point. The sub was designed to move across the seabed by means of two giant cogwheels, one fore and one aft. Power was supplied by a 30-horsepower gasoline engine whose fumes were vented to the surface through a 20-foot pipe, capable of being extended as needed; another pipe supplied fresh air.

Founded in 1815 as Baltimore Copper Smelting and Rolling Co., the 15-acre plant, pictured above in 1861, was a major industrial presence and job driver.

After the sub managed several test runs, Jules Verne, best-selling author of *"20,000 Leagues Under the Sea,"* sent *Argonaut* builder Simon Lake a congratulatory telegram.

Manufacturers aspiring to link up with the maritime chain crowded the waterfront area to reduce their transportation costs for incoming raw materials and outgoing finished goods. Ferries and small bridges connected busy sections of the port area. Vane Brothers chandlery opened in Fell's Point in 1898 as a one-stop provisioning shop for ships and crews; Vane dealt with the butcher, the baker, the ironmonger, and even the post office. Today, the company supplies an expanded range of services, and distributes fuel to the Eastern Shore and East Coast locales.

International giant McCormick Spice Company opened up shop in 1889. Today McCormick imports commodities from 35 nations through the Port of Baltimore to produce more than 15,000 products, more than two-thirds of which are made in Maryland. George Gunther began making beer with imported hops, one of 30 small area breweries at the time; Gunther developed a strong local following as an original sponsor of the Baltimore Orioles.

The Port provides, whether one aspires to sell several products or 15,000.

Right: Charles Hughes, Jr. in his family's ship chandlery in 1960. Vane Brothers, at the foot of Broadway in Fell's Point, provided all the essentials — including McCormick spices, inset — to mariners. Vane Brothers has left the chandlery business and focuses on bunkering and oil transportation.

In 1896, Congress authorized deepening the harbor channel to 35 feet. Bugeyes, pungies, sloops and schooners swarmed harbor piers to disgorge cargoes of Eastern Shore produce, which then were transported to area canneries, and finally packaged and distributed via the maritime chain's transportation network. As the level of commerce climbed higher, so did the numbers of advertising shops, hotels, banks and insurance companies, and steam-wagon manufacturers. Port activity expanded into the outer harbor, downriver to Curtis Bay and Patapsco Neck. Maryland's transportation network was tied into 33 states via the B&O.

The western ramp of the Francis Scott Key Bridge is anchored in Hawkins Point, an area with a long military history. Fort Armistead was built on Hawkins Point during the Spanish-American War in the late 1890s, and another river fort, Fort Carroll, was constructed in 1850 on a manmade island in the harbor offshore. Robert E. Lee, then an Army colonel, directed the effort. A World War II marine ammunition terminal was later bought by the Maryland Port Administration (MPA), which developed its Hawkins Point Terminal to serve industrial partners such as Grace Davison, a large producer of inorganic chemicals.

THE PORT PROVIDES, WHETHER ONE ASPIRES TO SELL SEVERAL PRODUCTS OR 15,000.

Baltimore City, feeling a bit crowded by all this growth, expanded from 10 to 30 square miles, as its northern boundary extended beyond Druid Hill Park. In 1900, Baltimore's population was 508,957, up from 169,000 in 1850. It was America's sixth most populous city. Only New York, Chicago, Philadelphia, St. Louis and Boston were larger.

Steamboats were in high season, jostling for freight and passengers at Light Street and Pratt Street piers in the Inner Harbor. In 1904, the first car reached Ocean City, Maryland. The advent of automobiles meant more roads, which provided stronger freight links to remote towns in the eastern and western parts of the

state, and a cure for what ailed their economic health via their new access to the Port's national and international markets. Residents of towns like Accident — located north of Oakland in Garrett County — enjoyed their first reliable connection to the National Road, which led to the Port of Baltimore.

And with more roads, there came more trucks, with ever-greater load capacities. It was a big change from the horse-and-buggy era, a development that increased business at the Port, where more products now were positioned to plunge into the maritime chain. The Canton Company built a 33-mile railroad to connect the Port's three trunk lines — the B&O, Pennsylvania and Western Maryland

Hawkins Point, at the foot of the Key Bridge, today provides terminal services for bulk carriers, such as this alumina ship. The electrically powered crane offloads cargo with its clamshell bucket and deposits it into railcars or trucks.

41

railroads — and constructed specialized bulk-shipping facilities such as an ore pier, sulphur bins and a nitrate shed while it organized subsidiaries for stevedoring and warehousing.

In 1908, Canton residents uncovered the charred remains of a 130-foot-long clipper ship buried 400 feet inland from the current shoreline that burned pierside; Canton's Cannery Row handled Shore produce — the Bay's oyster harvest peaked in 1884 at 15 million bushels — and pineapples from the Bahamas.

The Curtis Bay Towing Company, which specialized in handling bigger vessels, was founded just in time to capitalize on bulk carriers tied up at the new grain elevator built by the Western Maryland Railroad at Port Covington.

There's little to rival the compact horsepower and tenacity tugboats bring to the job: Curtis Bay was bought by Moran Towing in 1958. Moran has 13 locations from New Hampshire to Port Arthur, Texas. McAllister Towing, whose fleet straddles 10 East Coast ports and Puerto Rico, purchased Baltimore-based Baker-Whitely in 1980. Tugs, besides berthing and offshore operations, also have marine firefighting capability. America's oldest operating steam tugboat, the *Baltimore*, built at the Skinner yard in Fell's Point in 1906, is moored behind the Baltimore Museum of Industry.

24/7/365 x 300: The Port of Baltimore never sleeps. Its waterfront works night and day, in good weather and bad, like a 1950 snowstorm along Pratt Street in the Inner Harbor. Trucks provide drayage service at the Long Dock next to the city power plant. Today, the area is devoted to restaurants and other tourist attractions.

Right: Harbor tugs shift a newly launched tanker at Bethlehem Steel's Sparrows Point Shipyard. The white dot on the smokestack of the tug at the far left indicates it belongs to the Baker-Whitely fleet, while the diamond on the tug in the foreground is the insignia of Curtis Bay Towing.

Below: Moran Towing of New York purchased the Curtis Bay fleet in 1958. McAllister Towing, another New York firm, bought Baker-Whitely in 1980.

Big Steel

Sparrows Point Plant
BETHLEHEM STEEL COMPANY

Sparrows Point was still wide-open country when the Pennsylvania Steel Company, convinced the Dundalk peninsula would make a world-class deepwater port for its shipbuilding subsidiary, began its Baltimore operations in 1887 on the North Point parcel originally deeded to Thomas Sparrow by Lord Baltimore.

But giant Bethlehem Steel Company also coveted the site, and the closer America came to war, the more irresistible the plant seemed to Bethlehem President Charles Schwab, whose grand design was to make Sparrows Point the greatest steel-making machine known to mankind — all because of its proximity to the Port and the industrial transportation network which kept material moving through Maryland's maritime machinery.

Steel is made from iron ore, chrome ore and manganese ore, which are all imported. At Bethlehem's Pennsylvania site, ore had to be hauled from port to plant by rail. But Baltimore's tidewater location, with its deepwater access, had the potential to save the company $2 in manufacturing costs per finished ton of steel, and thus shift the balance of power toward Bethlehem Steel and away from competing Midwest steel works.

For $25 million, Bethlehem bought the plant in 1916 — and gained possession of its valuable ore reserves. Expansion began immediately. A new tin-plate mill was erected, and another $15 million was spent on a mill to produce steel plate for battleships and tanks. Greater batches of Beth Steel's components emerged from the Port's pipeline — plate steel for shipbuilding and construction,

Facing page: The proximity of Bethlehem Steel's shipbuilding yards to its steel furnaces and the coal and ore piers supplying imported raw materials created an industrial behemoth that provided work to tens of thousands of area residents. Bethlehem's other area facilities — its ship repair yard at Key Highway (above) and shipbuilding yard at Sparrows Point (left) — provided work for many thousands more.

Above, left: Bethlehem Steel produced cylinders used in construction of the Harbor Tunnel, as well as the Baltimore City fireboat *Torrent*, built in 1921. Above, right: *Torrent*, constructed partly in response to the devastating Great Baltimore Fire of 1904, inset, was stationed in Canton.

tin plate for canners and meatpackers, bar and sheet steel for the auto industry, steel rods for wire, springs and nails, and steel for rails and railroads.

Talk about Maryland's economic development! Fast forward to 1947: When four out of every five items manufactured in America contain steel, there are worse things in life than having the world's biggest steelmaker in your backyard, adjacent to a transportation hub where international supply and demand lines converge.

Baltimore's great fire of 1904 charred 140 acres, threw 35,000 people out of work and destroyed the downtown business district and most of Cheapside Wharf, the Inner Harbor's mercantile hub. Fortunately, the Port's plentiful lines of international trade kept

Maryland's diversified economy humming. American Crown Cork & Seal, which sold half the world's bottle caps during the 1930s, was expanding by tapping into Highlandtown and Canton's workforces to make an array of products supplying packers and canners along Boston Street's waterfront. Shipyards thrived, doing double duty handling steam and sail-powered boats. The Menzies family's long relationship with the Port had entered its second decade; founded in 1893, The Terminal Corporation today is a leading mid-Atlantic provider of logistics services like warehousing and transportation.

Black & Decker, founded in Baltimore in 1910, was then just another little contract machine shop tethered to the Port's supply line. In the early 1960s, nearly 5,000 manufacturers in metropolitan Baltimore were tied into the Port's international lines of commerce. Today, offshoring and the erosion of America's manufacturing base have enfeebled America's export base and contributed substantially to America's staggering trade imbalance. Black & Decker, a global leader in power tools, is among the handful of great American manufacturers still standing.

Ports ride the big shoulders of their workforce, the longshoremen. Nothing moves on the waterfront of Baltimore's public marine terminals without the support of the International Longshoremen's Association, founded in 1913. Baltimore's private marine terminals are moving in the opposite direction; their use of non-union labor has grown over the past three decades.

Ports are among the few remaining union and blue-collar bastions in America. If the longshoremen are not working, neither is the global supply chain, and as lean inventory management becomes the operating standard of an industrialized world economy, dockside shutdowns and slowdowns become the worst nightmare of the global trade community, fully capable of bringing nations large and small to their knees overnight.

Organized labor on Baltimore's waterfront has avoided corrupt work practices which have plagued other ports in the past, most notably New York.

The opening of the Panama Canal in 1914 enabled the Port to move westbound cargoes more cheaply and easily than its East Coast competitors up north, and also increased intercoastal traffic, resulting in more stopovers in Baltimore and more money in the pockets of area businesses.

Big ships generate significant business all along the waterfront whenever they dock — work for the longshoremen who handle cargoes and the stevedores who direct longshoremen, for bay pilots and tugboats who escort the ships, for chandlers and others who supply ships, and for repair and refueling — not to mention retailers patronized by ships' crews. Today's ships pay $3,000 to $7,000 a day for a berth at the Port, whose marketing department adds value by inducing customers to bring high volumes of cargo through Baltimore.

Longshoremen who "work a ship" in port perform one of the most hazardous and grueling jobs in America's workforce, whether unloading bananas by hand along Pratt Street's piers in 1945, left, or when operators of cranes and trucks, above, do much of the hauling.

Tin Men

Port traffic and the regional economy kept expanding. In 1920, state legislators authorized $50 million in loans to improve Port facilities, and federal funding was used to dredge the Patapsco and the Chesapeake's channels to the greater depth of 42 feet.

From 1914 to 1929, as demographics shifted toward urban areas, America's consumption of canned fruits and vegetables more than doubled. Eating food from tin cans, which were cheaper than glass containers, became the household norm. Sparrows Point was the only plant east of Pittsburgh producing all grades of tin plate. Demand for canned items soared, augmented by lithographic advances which made it possible to decorate papered cans with fancy advertising to appeal to upscale retail markets.

In turn, other lines of Baltimore-area businesses banded by the maritime chain profited — advertising, packing, paper producers, warehousing and ground transportation. The Tin Decorating Company of Baltimore — whose former factory anchors Tindeco Wharf in trendy Canton — was the largest tin decorating plant in the world when it opened in 1914, capable of producing four million tins daily. In 1955, 6,000 Marylanders were employed making tin cans.

The industry also made the product pitched by residential siding salesmen in Baltimore-born director Barry Levinson's film "Tin Men."

The last of the working sail-powered boats were seen around the Port after the turn of the 20th century, hauling up lumber from the Carolinas and Virginia, and transporting oysters and coal. As late as 1930, there were still 100 cargo schooners operating in the Bay. In the harbor's outer reaches — Curtis Bay, Canton and Patapsco Neck — clusters of military installations and utilities complemented investment by private industry to pack the Port area. The U.S. Coast Guard's only shipyard opened in Curtis Bay in 1899. Just up Curtis Creek, B&O built a mammoth $1.5 million coal pier.

The business of expediting the flow of cargoes through the maritime chain is the purview of freight forwarders and customs brokers: John S. Connor and Shapiro & Company both opened shop in Baltimore soon after the turn of the century, and have expanded their sea and airfreight operations to keep pace with the increasing complexities of international trade. The paperwork on a typical inbound shipment is staggering — hundreds of pages of customs regulations, thousands of tariff items, quotas, and multiple financial documents — while forwarders work to customize transportation door-to-door.

Facing page: Two U.S. Coast Guard cutters undergoing repairs at the Coast Guard Shipyard on Curtis Bay. Established in 1899, the facility is the only major repair yard operated by the Coast Guard. Above, left: Typical output of Port's maritime chain, both the product and its container.

The U.S. declaration of war on Germany in April 1917 renewed debate on the adequacy of America's maritime resources during global conflict. It took an extraordinary national effort for America's Merchant Marine fleet — which delivers troops and supplies during war, and also moves exports and imports in peacetime — to ramp up to speed in World War I. And even then, America was at the mercy of foreign ship operators who tripled their customary freight rate to transport U.S. military forces.

Troubled by this gap in America's national defense and the costliness of the short-term fix, two Marylanders took it upon themselves to ensure the nation wasn't caught short the next time. Bernard Baker, founder of Baltimore Storage and Lighterage (which became Baker-Whitely Towing), provided warehousing and merchandising for the Port community, tirelessly drove the government to build ships of U.S. registry and formed the International Mercantile Marine Company to help finance their construction. Maryland's U.S. Sen. George Ratcliffe worked the legislative end, introducing a bill that became the Merchant Marine Act of 1936.

In 1919, the Port of Baltimore ranked fifth among East Coast ports in foreign trade — tantamount to being in last place. Without the prospect of more cargoes, Baltimore couldn't attract more shippers. And vice-versa.

So the Export and Import Board of Trade and the Industrial Bureau of the Board of Trade (which subsequently merged to become the Baltimore Association of Commerce) hatched a plan to entice both industry and shipping simultaneously. To attract shippers, Baltimore put out the word that more industry was coming. And to get industry's attention, Baltimore announced that more shipping lines were on the way. The city boldly played both ends against the middle — and won. Both cargo tonnage and the steamship lines increased, the latter reaching 89 by 1955.

The lesson? Well-paying jobs and sustained economic growth don't materialize out of thin air. It took planning by Baltimore's business community — leaders intent on developing fully the Port's potential — to make it happen.

The next year, Baltimore's business leaders did it again. The Fidelity and Deposit Company of Baltimore, a leading national bonding and insurance agency, used the Port to showcase Maryland to America's financial community, and market the state to outside investors. In 1920, F&D organized a harbor tour for more than 3,000 top-ranked bankers, who boarded two excursion steamers in Locust Point, circled the upper and lower harbors, then proceeded down the Bay to Annapolis escorted by a U.S. Navy destroyer.

The tour was hailed as a stroke of visionary genius by Baltimore's newspapers, who editorialized about the long-term value of impressing national financial decision-makers.

On "Black Thursday," October 24, 1929, six weeks after peaking, the stock market plunged. The next week, on "Black Tuesday," the bottom dropped out of America's financial markets. If Maryland fared better than other states during the Great Depression, it generally has been attributed to the state's economic diversity, which issues from the Port.

IF MARYLAND FARED BETTER THAN OTHER STATES DURING THE GREAT DEPRESSION, IT GENERALLY HAS BEEN ATTRIBUTED TO THE STATE'S ECONOMIC DIVERSITY, WHICH ISSUES FROM THE PORT.

Facing page, far left: Covered lighterage barges — large, flat-bottomed vessels — protected cargoes in transit from ship to shed. Facing page, right: Seasonal produce was delivered under sail to Long Wharf at the Inner Harbor in 1936. Cargo booms assisted in offloading.

A ir travel was still a transportation frontier when Glenn L. Martin, already recognized as one of America's foremost airplane designers and builders, relocated his plant from Ohio to the Middle River area in 1930 to take advantage of the ready supply of raw materials deposited at his factory doorstep by the Pennsylvania Railroad.

Since runways were rare, the Bay's nearby waters proved just the place to test Martin's pontoon-equipped "flying boats." His seaplanes flourished as freight and passenger carriers, which enhanced Maryland's national reputation and economic prospects by attracting new industries. During World War II, the Martin plant was Maryland's second-largest defense contractor.

After the Harbor Tunnel leaves Canton and crosses under the middle branch of the Patapsco, it re-emerges in Fairfield, where one of America's mightiest feats of industrial performance began on April 30, 1941, when the keel of the *Patrick Henry* — named for the Revolutionary War patriot who said "Give me liberty, or give me death!" — was laid, the first of the 609 steel carriers in the armada launched from Bethlehem Steel's Fairfield and Sparrows Point yards during World War II.

Baltimore's shipbuilders, always at their best in times of urgent national demand, reached their fullest expression under the whip of shipyard boss John Macy "Jack" Willis during World War II. The *Patrick Henry* was the first of 388 Liberty ships launched from Fairfield, forming the trans-Atlantic "bridge of steel" carrying America's fight to oversea wartime theaters. During peak production, when Bethlehem's yards employed 47,000 workers, another new Liberty rolled down Fairfield's wooden seaways into the Patapsco every 24 hours. Bethlehem also made 94 of the faster Victory ships — which proved better suited for postwar commerce — in addition to landing craft

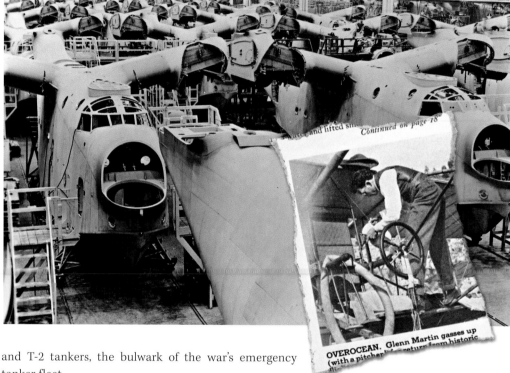

Continued on page 48

OVEROCEAN. Glenn Martin gasses up (with a pitcher...return from historic

and T-2 tankers, the bulwark of the war's emergency tanker fleet.

Bethlehem's final Fairfield tally is heavy with superlatives — a world shipbuilding record: the most ships and greatest tonnage of any wartime yard.

Maryland's economy was pre-positioned for wartime growth by the presence of the Port's infrastructure, and the state's superior transportation network, which was largely a byproduct of the Port. By August 1941, the value of just the previous 12 months of war-related business in Baltimore was $1.6 billion.

Baltimore's shipyards, besides building fast, new ships, were

Aviation pioneer Glenn L. Martin, inset, moved his aircraft manufacturing facility from Ohio to the Middle River, where his fame, payroll and "flying boats," top, took flight.

repairing torpedo-damaged ones. Glenn L. Martin's payroll soared from 3,500 to 53,000 on incoming orders from the Allies. Maryland's industrial machinery stepped up to supply everything from assemblies to debarkation nets. As in 1861 and 1917, clothing firms produced uniforms on a large scale for export. Companies in every line of work converted to supply wartime needs; Everedy Company in Frederick, which was using imported metals to make cutlery, started churning out anti-tank mines and rifle grenades.

Canton's postwar development began in 1946 when Rukert Terminals Corporation purchased Lazaretto Point from the Western Maryland Railroad. Founder Captain W.G.N. Rukert was a tough-talking waterfront character who cajoled McCormick founder Willoughby McCormick into selling Jackson's Wharf in Fell's Point in 1927; today, Rukert's maritime operations include 24 warehouses on 130 acres.

Baltimore's postwar port resembled an old warrior; many waterfront facilities had deteriorated beyond repair. Necessary modernization required a financial commitment that exceeded private-sector resources.

But Baltimore had other troubles. The Port's marriage to railroads, which had given them a transportation stranglehold on the waterfront and ownership of maritime terminals and other essential facilities, now worked against the Port's best interests by restricting trucking access to the waterfront. Baltimore was known as a "railroad port," its waterfront overly customized for railroads to handle bulk cargoes like wheat, coal and project cargoes, which served to drive general cargo business into the arms of competing ports. And the impending completion of the St. Lawrence Seaway, which would give New York a waterway to Midwest markets, posed another threat to Baltimore.

Above: Rukert Terminals now handles a variety of bulk cargoes, like the road salt area commuters see piled high along Interstate 95. Left: Of the hundreds of Liberty ships built in Baltimore during World War II, the last survivor is the *John Brown*, docked in Canton.

Maryland Port Authority

More fundamentally, the Port's competitive position was undermined by the absence of a dedicated oversight body empowered to coordinate the Port's operations, promote its growth and development, and provide public funds for modernization — the quasi-governmental, Port Authority-concept which had enabled rival ports to leapfrog over Baltimore.

Support for the value of a forceful public role in the Port's development acquired traction after a 1949 study undertaken on behalf of the Baltimore Association of Commerce, and picked up the weight of public opinion through early 1956, until state legislators — prodded by an intense lobbying effort from the business community's newly formed Greater Baltimore Committee — authorized the creation of the Maryland Port Authority, enabling it to build major public marine terminals using both its bonding power and the financial wherewithal of a 0.5 percent duty levied on profits of state corporations. Prime Port Authority movers including Maryland Gov. William McKeldin, GBC Chairman William Boucher, Baltimore's Junior Association of Commerce, Dr. Mildred Otenasek, *The Sun's* maritime voice, and State Roads Commissioner Robert O. Bonnell, Sr. finally could stop pushing.

The Port Authority moved decisively to transform Baltimore from a "railroad port" into a "shipper's port." Its signature move was the 1959 purchase of Baltimore's 356-acre Harbor Field airport tract which became the Dundalk Marine Terminal. In 1964, the Port Authority leased the B&O's Locust Point piers, signaling the railroad's acquiescence to the need to change Baltimore's waterfront modus operandi of the last 100 years.

The Port Authority soon managed other facilities at Canton and Clinton Street. Baltimore's waterfront acquired a sleek new face — modernized marine terminals like the Port Authority's first makeover, at Hawkins Point in 1958, a site which soon enticed corporate heavyweights like U.S. Gypsum Company and Kennecott Refining Corporation.

Vested with the independence to freely use its public revenue stream, the Port Authority worked to put Baltimore on equal footing with other major American ports. Foreign promotional offices were established, effectively championing the Port of Baltimore as an American point of entry. Dredging was needed to accommodate ever-bigger deepwater ships, and Baltimore, which enjoyed two access routes to the sea, had twice the need of other ports. The main channel was deepened to 42 feet and widened to 800 feet, a project that was no sooner completed when Congress authorized a deeper channel of 50 feet and up to 1,000 feet wide.

The 31-mile channel in the upper Bay connecting the Port to the C&D Canal was excavated to 35 feet, improving the strategically critical link handling New York's container ship traffic, which would otherwise dock in Virginia to save the time and expense of making the long run up to Baltimore after passing through Virginia's twin capes at the mouth of the Chesapeake.

What goes around, comes around: Maryland industries which owed their existence to Baltimore's waterfront and waterways were now instrumental in massive public works — such as the Harbor Tunnel and Bay Bridge — girding and connecting the very areas those waterways divided, creating an improved transportation network which, in turn, stimulated more commerce. Bethlehem's Sparrows Point shipyard and steel mill were major contributors to the tube built beneath Baltimore's harbor, completed in 1957. John Edwin Greiner first came to work as a draftsman for B&O in 1885; he rose to assistant bridge engineer before founding Baltimore's J.E. Greiner Company, which was the lead contractor on the 4.3-mile span across the Chesapeake completed in 1952.

Facing page: A seagull's view of the Chesapeake Bay Bridge. The 4.3-mile William Preston Lane Memorial Bridge linked Maryland's eastern and western shores upon its 1952 completion. Above, top: Baltimore's Harbor Tunnel on its opening day in 1957. Above: Bill Boucher was the first chairman of the Greater Baltimore Committee.

The world of maritime celebrates another anniversary in 2006 — the 50th year of a transportation innovation that dominates 21st-century global commerce.

Malcom McLean was a North Carolina trucking executive-turned-ship owner; one day while waiting for his truck to be unloaded onto a freighter, he realized the task would be simplified if the entire trailer, including its contents, was lifted onboard the ship. A standard dock crew of 22 men could handle 16 times more container tonnage per hour than loose cargo. Loading a ship by hand took days; dockworkers had to unpack and then carefully secure separate items down in the hold. Loading a ship with steel containers took but a fraction of the time, so transportation costs plummeted.

Not only did cargoes suddenly become a whole lot cheaper to ship, but vessels could make more trips, and the encased cargoes were better protected. More everyday items in the typical American household soon came from overseas; as the trickle of cheaper, foreign-made goods into the U.S. became a torrent, it tilted the national balance of trade.

By the mid-1960s, the derelict Inner Harbor had deteriorated into a public eyesore; Pratt Street's piers were cracked and left unpainted. By the 1970s, downtown Baltimore was stagnating, retailers dying off and tourist revenue almost nil. City fathers, desperate to burnish Baltimore's image, again looked to the same waterfront area where it all began 300 years before, and partnered with the Rouse Company to build Harborplace. Baltimore became the urban model; *Time* magazine dubbed it "Renaissance City." Structures which served the Port of generations past — an urban landscape of old warehouses and abandoned industrial sites — were rehabilitated and gentrified. The Scarlett Place condominiums replaced the old seed emporium; B&O's Camden warehouse became the administrative portion of the model sports palace, the new home of the Baltimore Orioles.

Above: The Maryland Port Administration is headquartered at the Inner Harbor's World Trade Center, foreground. Left: Seagirt Marine Terminal recorded a world-class 47 container "lifts" in March 2006. Malcom McLean, inset, invented the container and revolutionized the shipping industry. Facing page: Helen Delich Bentley christens the *Export Leader* in 1972.

Port Patrons

*D*uring the last 60 years, a handful of Maryland's Congressional delegation became recognized as the Port's patrons. More recently, three Maryland U.S. Senators — Barbara Mikulski, Paul Sarbanes and Charles "Mac" Mathias — helped bring home dredging funding, while three others enjoyed positions of leadership during the 1960s: George Fallon, who became chairman of the House Public Works Committee; Ed Garmatz, chairman of the House Merchant Marine Committee; and Sam Friedel, who chaired the House Administration Committee. And although they all thumped for the Port's best interests, none matched the high level of forceful advocacy dished out by Helen Delich Bentley, formerly maritime editor of *The Sun*.

Bentley, who served as Chairman of the Federal Maritime Commission from 1969 to 1975, became sufficiently aroused by delays in dredging Baltimore's 50-foot channel that she decided to challenge the re-election of the popular incumbent to the U.S. House of Representatives in 1980. Elected on her third try, Bentley pushed through legislation which enabled the work to be completed in 1989.

In 1971, a tough and tumultuous stretch for the Port was kicked off by a fit of legislative pique in Annapolis which subordinated the Maryland Port Authority under the newly created Maryland Department of Transportation, whereupon it was renamed the Maryland Port Administration.

Congressional deregulatory initiatives cut a wide swath through American industry during the last quarter of the 20th century. In 1980, the Staggers Rail Act signaled the onset of railroad deregulation; the Interstate Commerce Commission's power over rates and routes was curtailed, eliminating the differential

cost advantage Baltimore enjoyed over rival ports, which soon siphoned off business. Another source of revenue declined with the elimination of federal shipbuilding subsidies, which deprived the Port of business generated by U.S.-flag ship traffic required to make calls in Baltimore and all other North Atlantic ports.

Baltimore's "railroad port" was particularly sensitive to the wave of railroad consolidation, another consequence of the ICC's demise. The shakeout, disruptive in the short term, was more adverse long term: Baltimore lost its opportunity to be the only East Coast port served by three Class 1 rail carriers, and also was stung when the corporate headquarters of the Chessie System decamped for Florida.

Baltimore was in the thick of it as the railroad saga continued to play itself out during the decade. Conrail, created in 1976 as the central northeast hub, already served the Port. Then Chessie, born by the merger of the B&O and C&O in the 1960s, linked up with Seaboard to become CSX; at the same time, the Norfolk Southern, knowing CSX would deny it access to Baltimore on the tracks of Western Maryland Railroad, asked Maryland officials to petition the ICC to permit access to the Port. But at the eleventh hour, the powers that be in Annapolis decided not to petition the ICC, forfeiting the chance for three railroads.

(The Port was never better served than by the Western Maryland Railroad, which B&O acquired in 1973 after it was squeezed by Chessie. The Western Maryland had one purpose: it existed to serve Maryland and the Port, running between Baltimore and Hagerstown. Port Covington was the Port's best general cargo and grain terminal.)

Norfolk Southern never forgot its rude treatment. Management focused all their investment on the Port of Norfolk, and by 1985 rail container traffic from Baltimore to the Midwest had declined 24 percent — and increased 25 percent from Norfolk.

In 1986, members of Maryland's Congressional delegation prevailed in efforts to block Norfolk Southern's purchase of Conrail, moved by pleas from CSX that it would harm the Port. Conrail was subsequently divvied up between CSX and Norfolk Southern,

and there are those in Maryland's maritime community of the persuasion that Baltimore received the short end of that stick — Norfolk Southern has proven a willing business partner in many port cities, while Baltimore's container traffic remains curtailed by tunnel heights on CSX tracks, which constrains double-stacking.

Baltimore's primary container handling facility is Seagirt Marine Terminal, situated between Canton and Dundalk. Built on landfill deposits taken from the 1985 excavation of the Fort McHenry Tunnel, Seagirt's mammoth 125-ton cranes are guided by global positioning system satellite data to perform delicate container "lifts." Baltimore is the national leader in the average number of lifts per hour, a statistic that serves as a key industry measure of port efficiency, and helps market Baltimore.

There were other contentious issues threatening to destabilize the Port's commerce during the 1980s. Dredging consumed much of

the maritime community's energy: 1986 federal legislation changed the funding rules for routine — and highly costly — channel maintenance, and the channel up the Chesapeake, at approximately 150 miles, is the longest in America.

Under the new regimen, ports now were forced to share the costs with the federal government: Baltimore's share was 35 percent. And disposing of dredged material became more problematic. Environmental regulations specify placement of all dredged material, and Hart-Miller Island, the containment area for materials the U.S. Army Corps of Engineers excavates for the Port, is already at near capacity.

The Maryland Port Commission — six gubernatorial appointees serving three-year terms, chaired by Maryland's Secretary of Transportation — was created in 1988 to oversee the Maryland Port Administration.

Facing page: The Western Maryland Railroad was a good and true partner to the Port before being absorbed into CSX. Above, left: Norfolk Southern often runs unit trains (carrying one commodity), delivering farm equipment from the Midwest to Baltimore over a weekend. Above, right: A crane operator's view looking down on a ship.

"Working in the Rain"

A period of labor unrest was yet another problem: the Port had become known for not "working in the rain," exasperating both business leaders and former Gov. William Donald Schaefer, who brought in Helen Delich Bentley to mediate the dispute between the International Longshoremen's Association representing dockworkers and the Steamship Trade Association representing shippers. Bentley kept both sides talking during a successful marathon eight-week bargaining session.

In 1990, Baltimore ranked fifth nationally in total tonnage and was No. 2 in containerized cargoes in 1981, but as the limitations of the maturing container market became more evident, the Port acted on recommendations of a marketing study authorized by its Executive Director Tai Yoshitani and re-invented itself, adopting a niche strategy in 1996 which focused on vehicular traffic or "ro-ro" — automobiles, plus farm and other off-road equipment that rolls on and off ships under its own power — and forest products. BalTerm, a joint venture between Terminal Corporation and Logistec of Montreal, has dedicated, customized terminals for handling the Port's paper market.

In 2001, Baltimore business was buoyed to learn that Mediterranean Shipping Company, a world leader in container capacity, had agreed to call at Seagirt for another 10 years. The Port was an East Coast pioneer in securing long-term contracts with shipping companies.

To help capture more of the market, the Maryland Port Administration opened a new, dedicated ro-ro terminal at the old Maryland Shipbuilding and Drydock site in Masonville in 2002. Later that same year, in response to the 9/11 terrorist attacks, Congress passed the Maritime Transportation Security Act, which imposed a barrage of costly security measures on America's maritime community.

The Port scored another coup in 2003 when Mercedes-Benz inked a long-term lease to use its Fairfield terminal; Baltimore expects to process no less than one million Mercedes vehicles over the first 10-year lease period. By 2005, Baltimore was the national leader in ro-ro cargo, with more than 50 percent of the total U.S. market.

The Port continues to progress in the national rankings. In 2004, as record cargoes in excess of 8 million tons crossed its piers, Baltimore ascended to the seventh spot nationally in cargo value, and climbed to 14th in tonnage. Traffic increased in all targeted commodities — ro-ro, forest products, and containers — and Wallenius Wilhelmsen, the largest roll-on roll-off carrier in the world, chose Baltimore as its North Atlantic hub. With the groundbreaking for Baltimore's new cruise terminal in South Locust Point, an array of statewide businesses hope to benefit from an increased flow of passenger ships.

Facing page: In 2005, more than a half-million cars crossed Baltimore's piers. Top: The Port's state-of-the-art security technology scans containers. Above: The first VW bugs were discharged at Pier 6 on Pratt Street.

Greater Role

I n 2004, Baltimore City government gave maritime interests a key legislative victory by approving a city-wide zoning scheme which curbed the encroachment of deep-pocket developers on remaining deep-water parcels in the Port area. The Maritime Industrial Zoning Overlay District (MIZOD) delineates tracts off-limits for non-industrial purposes. More importantly, the legislation codifies Baltimore's commitment to protect the Port's best interests, recognizing that regulatory relief is a prerequisite for attracting the necessary level of maritime investment to sustain the region's economic growth.

Expediting the traditionally tedious approval process for a new dredge deposit site sits high on the Port's agenda. In February 2006, Baltimore's port welcomed the largest container ship to ever drop anchor in its harbor — the 900-foot long MSC *Tokyo*. Weighing 72,000 tons, the *Tokyo* was, in fact, one of Mediterranean Shipping Company's medium-sized vessels, carrying 5,600 TEU containers, while Mediterranean's biggest ships hold 9,200.

The Port's container traffic increased 12 percent in 2004-05, and Baltimore, unlike many other ports, has the potential to expand its container-handling capability. But as the industry trends towards ever-larger vessels, dredging issues could be a pending impediment in Baltimore's efforts to capture its share of the booming container traffic.

The Port of Baltimore, with a little legislative help from its friends, is positioned to play an even greater role in the future global world economy where supply and demand are increasingly served by one giant international market, instead of regional or national markets as in the past.

The winners in globalization's regime — in which increasingly more goods will be transported greater distances — are regions best-positioned to capitalize on inbound and outbound traffic of the global supply chain.

In the same way that old Baltimore Town was developed — block by block and pier by pier, radiating out from the Port's core — the sea lanes and transportation arteries which radiate out from Maryland's Port of Baltimore are the best bet to sustain the state's future economic development.

Whenever Maryland's economic security is called into question, one answer echoes down the halls of history to burst forth:

Facing page: Tugboats like the *Kaleen McAllister* work along Port piers.

Above: Line handlers help keep stacks of containerized cargoes, inset, moving through the Port's maritime chain.

The Port. It works … for 300 years and counting.

Sources

- Baltimore City Department of Planning: "The History of Baltimore," 2006
- Baltimore Sun, Sunday magazine; "The Port of Baltimore," January 9, 1955
- Baltimore Sun, Sunday magazine, "The Port of Baltimore," January 22, 1956
- Browne, Gary Lawson; "Baltimore in the Nation, 1789-1861," University of North Carolina Press, Chapel Hill, 1980
- Brugger, Robert J.: "Maryland: A Middle Temperament," Johns Hopkins University Press, 1988
- Chapelle, Baker, Esslinger; "Maryland: A History of Its People," Johns Hopkins University Press, 1986
- Hayward, Mary Ellen; "Maryland's Maritime Heritage," Maryland Historical Society, 1984
- "History of Baltimore," Lewis Historical Publishing Company, New York Chicago, 1912
- Keith, Robert C.: "Baltimore Harbor," Johns Hopkins University Press, 2005
- Living Classrooms Foundation, "The Rising Tides of Freedom" 2005
- Olson, Sherry H.: "Baltimore: the Building of an American City," Johns Hopkins University Press, 1997
- Peskin, Lawrence A.: "Fells Point: Baltimore's Pre-Industrial Suburb," Maryland Historical Society magazine, Summer 2002
- Reutter, Mark, "Making Steel," University of Illinois Press, 2004
- Rukert, Norman G.: "Federal Hill: a Baltimore National Historic District," Bodine & Associates, 1980
- Rukert, Norman G.: "Historic Canton: Baltimore's Industrial Heartland and Its People," Bodine & Associates, 1978
- Scharf, J. Thomas; "History of Baltimore City and County," Louis H. Everts, Philadelphia, 1881
- Sharp, Henry K.: "The Patapsco River Valley," Maryland Historical Society, 2001
- Television series "The Port That Built a City and State," WMAR-TV, 1950-1965
- Travers, Paul J.: "The Patspsco: Baltimore's River of History."

The Great Port of Baltimore: Its First 300 Years was published
for the Port of Baltimore Tricentennial Committee by: MEDIA TWO, INC.

PRESIDENT Jonathan Witty   ART DIRECTOR Darby Lassiter

PROJECT MANAGER Kim Fortuna   PHOTOGRAPHER/ Kathy Bergren Smith
                                  PHOTO EDITOR
MANAGING EDITORS Pete Kerzel
                 Blaise Willig

IMAGES

Painting on Cover by Patrick O'Brien

Photography by A. Aubrey Bodine
Copyright © Jennifer B. Bodine
- pg 1, Baltimore Harbor
- pg 8, Loading Tobacco
- pg 25, center: Fort McHenry
- pg 34, left: Buy Boat, right: Hampden-Woodberry Mill
- pg 42, Long Dock Baltimore Harbor
- pg 45, top right: Sparrows Point
- pg 46, left: Sparrows Point
- pg 47, bottom: Unloading Bananas
- pg 50, right: Melons at Long Wharf
- pg 58, Engine 828

Photography by Kathy Bergren Smith
All images are copyrighted by the photographer and may not be reproduced without express permission.
- pg 3 • pg 6 • pg 11, left • pg 12 • pg 15 • pg 16
- pg 17, center inset • pg 19 • pg 20
- pg 21, bottom inset • pg 24 • pg 28 • pg 30, top right
- pg 32, bottom • pg 33 • pg 36 • pg 38 • pg 40, inset
- pg 41 • pg 43, inset • pg 47, top • pg 48 • pg 49, left
- pg 53 • pg 54 • pg 56, top and bottom
- pg 59, left and right • pg 60 • pg 61, top
- pg 62 • pg 63, top inset and top

Photography by A.R. Jordan
All images are copyrighted by the photographer and may not be reproduced without express permission.
- pg 11, center and right • pg 53, bottom inset

Photography courtesy of The Baltimore Fire Department Marine Division, Fireboat #1
- pg 46, right, Fireboat #1

Photography courtesy of The Baltimore Museum of Industry
All images are copyrighted by the museum and may not be reproduced without express permission.

- pg 7 • pg 10, bottom left and right • pg 13, top
- pg 14, right • pg 21, top
- pg 22, first and second image from left
- pg 23, first and fourth image from left
- pg 26, top right • pg 27, top right
- pg 29, bottom and inset • pg 30, bottom
- pg 31, bottom inset • pg 35 • pg 37, inset
- pg 39 • pg 43, right • pg 44
- pg 45, top and bottom insets • pg 50, bottom left
- pg 52, top and bottom inset • pg 55, top

Photography courtesy of The Greater Baltimore Committee
- pg 55, bottom inset

Photography courtesy of The Dundalk Historical Society
- pg 52, center • pg 61, bottom inset

Photography courtesy of Helen Delich Bentley
- pg 57

Photography courtesy of The Library of Congress
- pg 10, center, bottom inset • pg 13, center • pg 18
- pg 22, fourth from left • pg 23, third from left
- pg 25, top inset • pg 26, bottom inset
- pg 31, top right • pg 32, top inset • pg 46, top inset

Photography courtesy of The Maryland Historical Society, Baltimore, Maryland
All images are copyrighted by the museum and may not be reproduced without express permission.
- pg 3, background image • pg 9
- pg 13, bottom right inset • pg 14, bottom left inset
- pg 17, top and bottom postcard images
- pg 22, third from left • pg 23 fourth from left
- pg 25, bottom inset • pg 27, center and bottom inset
- pg 29, top inset and top right • pg 49, top right

Photography courtesy of Vane Brothers
- pg 40, left